"In *Setting Up Your Scenes*, Pepperman takes a great approach. He presents the reader a track to further film exploration. Many of the films selected amount to some of my favorites. Others I've not heard of nor seen. I like when a book takes me to — or shows me — new things."
— Larry J. Hillier, Cinematographer;
Film & Video Production Teacher

"It looks like another winner from Michael Wiese Productions. It's one of those thump-yourself-on-the-head-I've-been-waiting-for-this books. It presents 'scene studies' of classic US and foreign films spanning sixty years. It's surely a godsend for students, although the fresh approach will have wider appeal for anyone interested in making DV movies."
— Derek Pell, Editor, *www.dingbatmag.com*

"Richard Pepperman has inspired hundreds of film students. This book is a treasure of his many years of experience. *Setting Up Your Scenes* raises the teaching of filmmaking to a higher level. This book may become to film students what *Gray's Anatomy* is to art students. If form and content matter, this book is required reading!"
— Tony Ceglio, Former Director of Broadcasting:
N.Y. Football Giants; Founder & CEO, Italian
American Channel, Multiple Emmy Winning
Producer & Director

"Richard Pepperman de-mystifies the filmmaking process, breaking down individual scenes from a great selection of movies. *Setting Up Your Scenes* helps the reader understand the motivations behind each camera angle [that] the director and editor have chosen for the final form. Being able to 'read' through a [scene] shot by shot is an excellent learning tool for beginning filmmakers. The language of cinema is clearly explained, and beautifully organized in Pepperman's book."
— Melissa Shachat-Edmon, Award-Winning
Documentary Director; *Living A Full House* and
Gibtown

"My dear colleague has challenged the film teaching community — and himself — yet again, by writing a second book on how to explain the unexplainable of filmmaking. And again, he did it! Richard knows quite well that before one goes deep one should go wide."
— Zoran Amar
a.k.a. Grandfather Film (a name given by his SVA
Film Students), Film Production & AVID Teacher

"In *Setting Up Your Scenes*, Richard Pepperman illustrates the creative choices made by directors in constructing enjoyable and meaningful movies. Through a dissection of scenes from diverse films, Pepperman reveals the way to effective scene structure, its importance in the overall film and its effect upon an audience. Here is a book for all filmmakers and screenwriters."
— Howard Beckerman, Animator, teacher and
author of *Animation: The Whole Story*

"*Setting Up Your Scenes* gets to the very core of great directing — combining compelling shots to tell a story with pictures. This gloriously detailed examination of scene construction is a must for those serious about the craft of directing."
— Chris Gore, author of *The Complete DVD Guide*
and editor of *Filmthreat.com*

"Pepperman's instructive voice, which is clear, knowledgeable and enthusiastic, comes across in his writing style. This book is as good as an entire course in film studies; and provides a great resource for film students and teachers alike."
— JoJo Whilden, Filmmaker & Photographer

"Pepperman dissects some very infamous scenes from some very famous movies – providing us with the most breathtaking black-and-white stills – in order to highlight the importance of the interplay between dialogue, subtext, and shot selection in great filmmaking. The beauty of this work is that while it will teach anyone who is willing to learn, it works equally well as a gorgeous coffee table book for the unwilling amongst us."
— Lily Sadri, Screenwriter, *Fixing Fairchild*

"*Setting Up Your Scenes: The Inner Workings of Great Films* is truly a priceless book for any student of film or novice just making his or her way into the industry. But it is also priceless for anyone who has been working in the biz for awhile who may have forgotten, amidst worries of marketing and box office and demographics, the sheer emotional power of a great scene that stays with you long after you have left the darkened theater."
— Marie Jones, Book Reviewer, *www.absolutewrite.com*

"The breadth and depth of examples, and the numerous illustrations in *Setting Up Your Scenes*, speak to all of us visual learners. Pepperman's x-rays of scenes convey clearly and quickly the ways a director's choices guide and impact the viewer. Every filmmaker will benefit from the insightful analysis carefully presented."
— Diane Carson, Ph.D., Professor of Film Studies, St. Louis Community College at Meramec

"Pepperman has written a book which should form the basis for an intelligent discussion about the building blocks of great scenes across a wide variety of films. Armed with the information in this book, teachers, students, filmmakers, and film lovers can begin to understand how good editing and scene construction can bring out the best storytelling to create a better film. It's well known that understanding editing can improve every filmmaker's work. This book provides a great starting point to grasp what that phrase really means."
— Norman Hollyn, Associate Professor and Editing Track Head, School of Cinema-Television, University of Southern California and author of *The Film Editing Room Handbook: How to Manage the Near Chaos of the Cutting Room*

"If I'd had access to Richard Pepperman's *Setting Up Your Scenes* ten years ago, it could have quite possibly saved me $100,000 in film school fees, not to mention a lot of time and grief. This book is a must-have for all would-be filmmakers and screenwriters."
— Far Dada, Independent Filmmaker, Toronto, Canada

"Richard Pepperman's latest book, *Setting Up Your Scenes*, is not only visually stunning but also a very useful book for students of cinema. Its design, layout, and content make the book unique and irresistible."
— Amresh Sinha, New York University/The School of Visual Arts

"I have been waiting many years for a book like this to come along. Other than making our own films and learning from our mistakes, I can't think of a better way to learn the secrets of effective filmmaking than deconstructing classic films. Film professors have traditionally done just that and they know how much students benefit from it. Great scenes can teach us so much about effective screenwriting, building dramatic tension, controlling editorial rhythm and pacing, blocking, composition and directing performance. In this book, Richard Pepperman, a very accomplished editor and teacher, has done the legwork for us, sharing the secrets of those incredible scenes from the classic films we know and love."
— Dave Porfiri, Independent Filmmaker; Professor of Film and Media Arts, American University, Washington, DC

"As an actor my concern is to be in the moment to bring the scene to life, sometimes feeling adrift in the swirl of the bigger picture. *Setting Up Your Scenes*, a beautiful book by Richard D. Pepperman, seduces me with extraordinary image and text to understand the scene as a whole. Exquisitely designed by Gina Mansfield and expertly written by Pepperman, whose passion for film embraces every page, *Setting Up Your Scenes* will enrich any movie lover's collection; even actors."
— Cathy Haase, Actress, Author of *Acting for Film*

SETTING UP YOUR SCENES
THE INNER WORKINGS OF GREAT FILMS

RICHARD D. PEPPERMAN

Published by Michael Wiese Productions
11288 Ventura Blvd., Suite 621
Studio City, CA 91604
T: 818.379.8799
F: 818.986.3408
mw@mwp.com
www.mwp.com

Cover Design: Michael Wiese Productions
Layout: Gina Mansfield
Editor: Paul Norlen

Frame Grabs: Post It Media
Film & Video Editing/Sound Design/Web Design
www.postitmedia.com
Adriana Alfieri
Eric Ramistella

Printed by McNaughton & Gunn, Inc., Saline, Michigan
Manufactured in the United States of America

Library of Congress Cataloging-in-Publication Data

Pepperman, Richard D., 1942-
  Setting up your scenes : the inner workings of great films / Richard D. Pepperman.
      p. cm.
  Filmography: p.
  ISBN 1-932907-08-4
  1. Motion pictures--Plots, themes, etc. 2. Cinematography. 3. Motion pictures--Philosophy. I. Title.
  PN1997.8.P44 2005
  791.43'01--dc22

                                        2005006811

For Betsy

New technologies, at bargain prices, make it possible for (nearly) anyone to become a competent filmmaker — a democratic global Hollywood. But! Democracy's utmost bequest is that great art is accessible to nearly everyone. Don't fail to take full advantage!

— rdp

CONTENTS

ACKNOWLEDGMENTS

The inspiration for this book came from Jeremy Vineyard's *Setting Up Your Shots: Great Camera Moves Every Filmmaker Should Know* — an appealingly simple guide book — and from ideas stirred and encouraged by Michael Wiese; corroborated, added to, and kept on message by Ken Lee; and confirmed by several students and colleagues in the Film, Video & Animation Department at the School of Visual Arts. I thank them for paying attention to my early-scattered thoughts, for their always-constructive criticisms, and for all their valuable suggestions.

A grand "thank you" to Adriana Alfieri and Eric Ramistella, partners at Post It Media, New York City. They flawlessly followed my long list of shot descriptions; brilliantly duplicating the selected frames which produced the 400 movie stills situated throughout the book.

An appreciative acknowledgment must go to Internet Movie Data Base (IMDb), *www.imdb.com*; *Film & Video Companion 2004*, compiled by the editors of *TV Guide Online's* CineBooks Database; Barnes & Noble Books, New York; and *TLA Video & DVD Guide: The Discerning Film Lover's Guide 2004* (David Bleiler, editor, St. Martin's Griffin Press, New York). They provided essential information on cast and crew, characters, dates, distributors, production companies, and useful hints for simple story synopses.

I am happy to have worked again with text editor Paul Norlen. I thank him for his sustained smart work on my behalf. Paul is especially swift, clever, and a very wise "mender." Add to this his courteousness, and Paul turns out to be a literary ambassador — a most cultured attaché.

For a second time I am delighted to thank designer Gina Mansfield. Her many creative touches add up to absolute beauty.

ABOUT THIS BOOK

Filmmaking is a *backward* art form. Not as in "its place in history," but in the lessons it provides the artist. There's no better way to grasp — and appreciate — the required creative skills of the screenwriter, cinematographer, actor, editor, producer, director, and all the many others in film's collaborative process than to view a *completed work*. When all is done (and said) you can more easily "see" what went wrong, and right, and learn from both.

In the *end*, every choice decided upon, experienced and examined, can teach the filmmaker about every next *beginning*.

The purpose of this book is to take a backward look — with the spotlight on "what went right!"

The enclosed template will guide you through simple, yet jam-packed, **scene studies**. Here, in word and image, is an arrangement to help you understand how *scenes* are *set* by way of **story**, **characters**, **dialogue**, **scene value** (text and subtext), and **set-ups**. Then! How *great choices* bring them all together to produce a great scene: the Inner Workings of Great Films.

History & Genre

The films I've chosen may not be ones you'd likely line up to see. Perhaps there are titles you've not heard of. The selections give confirmation — and express my conviction — that filmmaking is an art form of vitality, and prestige.

I ask you to consider that great art expects more from *you*; and that there is nothing wrong with having to put in some genuine "work" at understanding. I confidently can promise that great work delivers great pleasure and satisfaction.

I have selected scenes from around the world — they cover six decades and offer a brief history in (*movie*) time — and located them in categories outside the usual genre listings. Scenes within a film may demonstrate qualities at odds with their genre: A *thriller* can contain a scene of *comedy*; a *comedy* might have a scene of *horror*. So, rather than *comedy*, *thriller*, *horror*, etc., I have set the scenes under the categories *Dangers*, *Delights*, *Exploits*, and *Attractions*.

Categories

While these categories identify the overall "feel" of selected scenes, they are not immune to the interconnectedness of sensations. I have situated the "Eating" scene from *Tom Jones* under *Attractions: The lustfulness of Tom and Mrs. Waters* for each other. But, with all of this scene's delectable foodstuffs it could certainly be located under *Delights*. In fact, given the *context* of previous moments — Mr. Fitzgerald's pursuit of Tom, suspecting that he's *bedding* Mrs. Fitzgerald; and Tom's earlier rendezvous in the woods — it could be argued that "Eating" fits all Categories!

I chose my categories because they better echo wider variations within a genre: *Dangers*, of course, cover suspense, horror, and thriller; *Delights* express comedy and enchantment; *Exploits* is likely adventure, and *Attractions* convey romance and desire. Most crucial of all, the categories signal an overall feeling, and quickly concentrate the scene's *dedicated sentiment* and emotional life:

Dangers: hazard; jeopardy; menace; peril; risk; threat.

Delights: enchantment; enjoyment; happiness; take pleasure in; satisfaction.

Exploits: bold stroke; deed of derring-do; feat; make use of; utilize.

Attractions: allure; appeal; enticement; seduction; temptation.

Scene Presentation
The Template
Each scene, in each category, is explored through a scene's indispensable *elements*.

Story provides a synopsis — in brief — to help set the overall storyline, plot, or premise of the film.

Scene @ 0:00:00 locates — in running time — when the scene appears.

Interior/Exterior. Location. Day/Evening/Night sets the place/time: Where the scene is located, and when.

Defining Scenes
I have taken license with the term **scene** as (technically) defined in production: *Continuous Time* in a *Consistent Location* from its first frame to its last.

To determine a *scene* I am making use of *dramatic structures* in topic, inflection, and beats.

In "Who Fired That Shot" from *Dog Day Afternoon*, I am including several *Interior* areas of the bank, as well as several *Exterior* areas on the Brooklyn street, but from the opening frame to the closing frame there is a well-defined form in dramatic structure.

In "Just Testing" from *Children of a Lesser God*, I am ending the scene — as technically defined — early, but at a clear and significant change in *topic*, *inflection*, and *beat*.

"Platypus" from *Burnt by the Sun* happens to conform both to my taking license and the technical definition of a *scene*.

A study of all the various *scene configurations* will provide extra exploration and learning.

A "Title" is offered as a point of *dramatic reference*: When editing, or working with students, I try to give a name to each scene, because its number — as in Scene 63 — holds neither context nor emotion; and therefore no strength of recollection.

What We Watch

Character(s) is a listing of the people who appear in the scene. For the most part, *they* are what an audience is most interested in watching.

Watch closely for the *activities* of each *character*.

Let me alert you to the basic three:
1. *Physical Action*: movement in the place or space.
2. *Physical Life*: the use of objects.
3. *Dialogue*: I have transcribed *words spoken* from the final release of the films. I did not venture to guess the original written dialogue; but in all likelihood some *words* have changed from the original screenplay.

All three help to determine the *coverage* in **set-ups**: How many angles, and how often (in takes) the three are repeated over — and over — again during production.

Scene Meaning & Worth

Scene Value takes a look at a scene's purpose and objective: the *Distribution of Information* in **text** and **subtext**. Most especially, how a scene joins with other scenes and sequences to add information that moves the story forward: Watch for connections, contrasts, obstacles, consequences, and resolutions that initiate new contrasts, obstacles, etc.

Storytelling Tools

Dramatic Irony and *Irony*: Essential to the thinking/feeling — full engagement — response in an audience.

Dramatic Irony: What an audience knows, or is aware of, that a character doesn't know, misunderstands, or misinterprets.

Irony: Paradox, incongruity, quirk of fate. (More "fashionable" — and *juvenile* — usage consists of sarcasm, mockery, and insincerity).

Coverage

Set-Ups is a *directory* of compositions in *scene* coverage. Each is situated on a continuum from (Extreme) Long Shot to (Extreme) Close-up.

When you watch a scene you are seeing the final selections in frame to frame construction. That is, lots of the frames exposed in the camera, and printed, are not in the finished film. For better teaching and learning, I have made "educated guesses" to determine what might have been the content of *full* camera runs.

So, for example, in "Melon" from *The Day of the Jackal*, the final form of the scene initiates one of its cuts in a Medium Shot on the Jackal's legs as he makes his way to a tree from which to sight his rifle, but the *set-ups* directory contains the (very likely) *previous* actions of the Jackal in Long Shot walking toward the camera, *arriving* into the Medium Shot.

Distinctions in Coverage

From scene to scene you will certainly notice extraordinary differences in the number of set-ups. Some scenes will be *covered* with dozens, while others with less than half a dozen. The number and variety is, in large part, a response to the number of characters, the location (the total area of *place* and *space*), and the complexity of movement and action.

Make yourself aware of well-motivated and well-paced camera moves: zooms, tilts, pans, and dollies.

The Finished Scene

The sorting and blending of shot compositions — and *selections in audio* — provide the scene's **Great Choices.** I encourage you to watch the films in their entirety — using this book as a guide — so that the context of the scenes can be valued; and to insure your appreciation of the emotions shaped by image and sound.

Images

Each entry contains images — from five to more than twenty — "pulled" from their scenes. These movie stills (more than 400 in all) are located under different elements within each template. Just as I've utilized the mood, tone, and dramatic content of a scene to determine its inclusion in category, I have positioned the images similarly: The movie stills appear wherever (I felt) they would best reveal the craft and creativity of the filmmakers, and the emotional life of the scene.

HOW TO USE THIS BOOK

The filmmaking process is traditionally divided into three phases: preproduction, production, and postproduction. The template for each entry is organized to facilitate a scene study in this order. Each scene can easily be examined with the three phases in mind.

Story, *Scene Location*, and *Dialogue* correspond to preproduction; *Scene Value*, *Text*, *Subtext*, and *Set-Ups* correspond to production; *Great Choices* represent the first two phases realized in postproduction.

It is worth considering the influence of each phase on the others, and their expected relationship throughout the filmmaking process.

The Director must recognize this as he, or she, works to:
1. Prepare the Screenwriter's work in preproduction.
2. Design a shot list with the assistance of the cinematographer, bringing preproduction to production.
3. Collaborate with the editor in the postproduction search for the "best" moments from the production material, so as to create a clear and engaging structure.

Getting Started

Before watching a scene:
1. Review the brief synopsis so as to grasp the fundamental story ideas.
2. Set the location in your mind — as your mind's eye visualizes it — from the *Scene* information. You should also take into

account how many minutes (or hours) into the film the scene occurs: This will have an impact on *Scene Value*.

3. Try to add the *characters* into your mind's eye vision of the scene. Make use of the movie stills (images) to stir your mind's eye!

4. Read the *dialogue*. Where there is *no* dialogue, try to visualize the actions you'd create for the *characters* from the story synopsis, and the distribution of information expressed in *Scene Value*.

5. Re-read the dialogue, combining the words with *your* visualized place and characters.

6. From your visualization of the full scene, draw up a list of the set-ups your mind's eye constructed for scene coverage.

Now screen the scene:

1. Compare the similarities and differences between your visualization and the actual scene.

2. Now review the directory of *Set-Ups* to evaluate the production similarities and differences.

3. What are the *Great Choices* that *your* visualization intuitively created?

4. Use the *Assignments for Discussion* found in *Added Attractions*.

I'll say no more. Enjoy your Scene Studies!

DANGERS

STORY

The two famous train robbers on the run from a relentless posse.

SCENE

@ 0:33:04

Exterior. Train. Day.

"Box Car Posse"

CHARACTERS

Butch

Sundance

Gang Members

Passengers

Pinkerton Posse

DIALOGUE

BUTCH
(*after setting explosives to blow the train's safe*)
Well, that oughta do it!

(*an explosion rips the safe, the boxcar… and then some*)
(*money fills the sky; the gang gathers it up as it floats to earth*)

SUNDANCE
Think you used enough dynamite there Butch?
(*laughs…laughs…laughs*)
(*another train approaches from far off*)

BUTCH
Now, what the hell is that?
(*boxcar door slides open; the posse springs out*)
Whatever they're selling I don't want it!
(*Butch, Sundance, and their gang flee*)

SCENE VALUE

This is the scene that sets the story's essential "adventure/escape" plot: It introduces the Pinkerton Posse, Butch and Sundance's antagonist.

TEXT
A wisecracking repartee — merriment in tone: Exhilaration following the enormous explosion and lots of money "dropping" from the sky.

SUBTEXT
A very early scene involving Butch's "scan" of a town bank "illustrated" that new devices and measures had arrived in the West. Increased security added enormous risk to bank robbery.

The "Box Car Posse" scene reinforces earlier revelations: Butch and Sundance's world has changed.

EXTREME LONG-SHOT
Butch, Sundance, and Gang Members wait outside the train.
An explosion tears the baggage car apart.

EXTREME LONG-SHOT
Wrecked box car, gang members, and approaching Posse Train.

LONG-SHOT
From behind Butch and Sundance. The baggage car explodes.

LONG-SHOT
Butch and Sundance fall to ground amid smoke and debris.

LONG-SHOT
Looking up to the sky as money floats about.

LONG-SHOT
Long Focal Length Lens: Posse Train smoke approaching.

LONG-SHOT
Posse Train approaches through the haze.

LONG-SHOT
Low-Angle. Boxcar door slides open, and the Posse leaps
from the train.

MEDIUM-SHOT
Butch moves to screen right alongside Sundance.

MEDIUM-SHOT
Butch and Sundance on the ground. They get up to their knees.

MEDIUM-SHOT
Butch and Sundance get up, and look to the sky.

MEDIUM-SHOT
Gang Member #1 grabbing falling money.

MEDIUM-SHOT
Gang Member #2 grabbing falling money.

MEDIUM-SHOT
Butch walks to train and picks up his hat.

MEDIUM-SHOT
Butch spots the Posse Train.

MEDIUM-SHOT
Long Focal Length Lens: Posse Train approaches.

MEDIUM-SHOT
Sundance moves alongside Butch. Together they watch
the approaching Posse Train.

MEDIUM-SHOT
Posse Train comes into **Close-Up**.

MEDIUM-SHOT
Posse Train pistons.

MEDIUM-SHOT
Smoking stack of Posse Train.

MEDIUM-SHOT
Posse Train boxcar. The door slides open.

MEDIUM-SHOT
Butch and Sundance turn to escape.

MEDIUM-SHOT
Low-Angle shot of boxcar. Door opens, the Posse leaps out.

MEDIUM-SHOT
Posse leaps over camera and rides toward Butch and Sundance.

MEDIUM-SHOT
Posse Train whistle zoom-in to **Extreme Close-Up**.

MEDIUM CLOSE-UP
Door of boxcar slides open.

CLOSE-UP
Posse Train engineer "window." It's empty.

CLOSE-UP
Posse Train front from Low-Angle.

CLOSE-UP
Butch and Sundance watching — waiting!

CLOSE-UP
Sundance putting on his hat. Camera follows as he bends to collect money.

CLOSE-UP
Sundance sees the Posse Train, and moves to screen left.

CLOSE-UP
Gang Member #1 sees the Posse Train.

CLOSE-UP
Gang Member #2 sees the Posse Train.

GREAT CHOICES

It's a "safe" guess that multiple cameras were set up to "cover" the explosion of the baggage car. Events that are difficult — or dangerous — to recreate are best filmed (with hidden cameras) simultaneously from a variety of angles and distances.

There's a wonderful contrast between the merriment following the explosion and the "mystery train" approaching. That contrast is enhanced in the audio. Boom! Quiet! Laughter! Quiet! The audio **beats** then play the emerging **suspense**:

"Time" implemented by the chug! chug! of the approaching Posse Train: There is great success in the varied visuals which bring the Posse Train down the tracks, closer and closer to Butch and Sundance.

The reactions of Butch, Sundance, and gang members create **beats** in mystery and anticipation.

The empty engineer "window" and other Posse Train mechanisms indicate a mystery/ghost train.

These images then "link up" with the audio when the train whistle (with fast zoom-in) pierces the air (and the ear), as a signal "tearing" open the Posse's boxcar door!

There is a perfectly timed "pause" before the Pinkerton Posse leaps from the boxcar: The door slides open showing a "vacant space."

The "Boxcar Posse" scene maintains the film's overall atmosphere of audacious jesting. This tone is likely the reason that the filmmakers ended the film with a **freeze frame** of Butch and Sundance — still on their feet — rather than a lifelike depiction of their deaths in a shootout in Bolivia, South America.

STORY

Tony Wendice arranges to have his wife murdered. The plot is precise, and (nearly) foolproof.

SCENE

@ 0:42:09

Interior. Men's Club/ Wendice Apartment. Night.

"Telly Plot"

CHARACTERS

Tony Wendice

Margot Wendice

Killer

Man in Phone Booth

MARGOT
(picking up telephone)
Hello? Hello? Hello!

SCENE VALUE

This is the "murder for hire" played out; but not exactly as planned.

SUBTEXT

With all the careful planning, many obstacles arise from the unexpected and unforeseen: This portends a series of remarkably clever twists.

SET-UPS

EXTREME LONG-SHOT

Bedroom door opens. Margot enters the dark living room, goes to the desk, and picks up the phone. The killer comes up behind her.

LONG-SHOT

Tony approaches the phone booth in the lobby. The camera pans right revealing that another patron is using the single phone booth. Tony waits "patiently." The caller leaves, and Tony enters the booth and dials up his wife.

LONG-SHOT

Killer is about to leave the apartment when "the call" comes in. He looks toward the bedroom, and moves back to his hiding place.

LONG-SHOT

Margot awakes to phone ringing. She gets out of bed. The camera follows panning left. Margot exits the bedroom, going into the living room.

LONG-SHOT

Margot at desk, on the telephone. The killer comes up behind her. She begins to hang up the phone. The killer strikes with the twisted scarf. Margot and killer struggle around the desk…

LONG-SHOT

The killer puts the scarf around Margot's neck. They struggle around the desk. Margot falls onto the desk, reaches back, grabs scissors, and stabs the killer. He stands, slumps, and then stands again. Margot falls to the floor.

LONG-SHOT

Killer struggles to reach the scissors sticking into his back.

MEDIUM LONG-SHOT

Angle from the floor. The killer is "dead-still." Margot pulls herself up to reach for the hanging telephone.

MEDIUM-SHOT

The Killer's POV (Point of View): Light appears under the bedroom door.

MEDIUM-SHOT

Killer struggles to reach the scissors stuck into his back.

MEDIUM-SHOT

Margot struggles, and falls back onto the desk. She reaches back and finds a pair of scissors. She swings them over and into the back of the killer. The camera tilts upward as the killer stands rigidly upright. The killer then slumps onto Margot.

MEDIUM-SHOT

Margot's legs and bare feet "struggle."

MEDIUM-SHOT

Margot comes to the desk, picks up the telephone. The camera dollies left around her, ending behind her. The killer's hands, holding a twisted scarf, appear from the frame's bottom.

MEDIUM-SHOT

From in front of Margot. She comes to the desk, picks up the telephone. The killer appears behind her. His strangling scarf at the ready. He waits for the telephone to be out of the way of Margot's neck. He brings the scarf over Margot's head and around her neck...

MEDIUM-SHOT

From the side. Margot is on the telephone. The killer comes up behind her. As Margot begins to hang up, the killer strikes....

CLOSE-UP

Looking down to Margot struggling on the desk. She reaches behind her for scissors, and brings them over and into the killer's back.

CLOSE-UP

Margot on the floor near the desk. She looks up at the stabbed killer, then looks away.

CLOSE-UP

Tony enters the booth, telephones Margot, and then listens to the struggle in the living room.

CLOSE-UP (TIGHTER)

Tony dials Margot, and listens in on the attempted murder.

CLOSE-UP

Telephone equipment at "work" as mechanical switches direct Tony's call.

EXTREME CLOSE-UP

Telephone dial on "MN6." A finger enters the frame, and the dial "opening," and turns the dial wheel.

EXTREME CLOSE-UP

Killer falls onto the floor, pushing the scissor blade deeper into his back.

Tony's watch has stopped, and he is now *late* telephoning Margot; a crucial element in the murder plot.

He hurries to a telephone booth, but it is occupied!

When Tony gets to use the "telly," the tension is brilliantly applied with an image of:

The inner workings of the telephone company "switching" mechanisms.

The call goes through, ringing the Wendices' home phone, just a *beat* before the Killer gives up waiting.

The Killer goes back to his hiding place. Margot picks up the "telly." Tony remains silent on the other end.

Here is an extraordinary moment of "I can't watch" suspense: The Killer cannot wrap the scarf around Margot's neck *until* she puts the phone down!

Then! Just as the deadly plot seems to be moving ahead as planned…

… Margot gets hold of a scissors.

"Telly Plot" is a perfect example of the difference between *horror* and *suspense*. Alfred Hitchcock himself described the difference this way: "If a character is walking down a hall, and someone leaps out of a closet with a knife, that's *horror*; but if, when a character walks down a hall, the audience *knows* that someone is in the closet with a knife, it's *suspense*." The audience's knowing is *Dramatic Irony*.

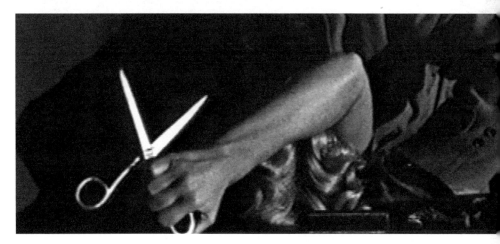

STORY

A hunch surveillance by two New York detectives uncovers a "deal" to purchase heroin being smuggled into the city from Marseilles, France.

SCENE

@ 0:02:24

Exterior/Interior. Marseilles Streets / Building Hallway. Day.

"Meet Frog Two"

CHARACTERS

French Undercover Detective

Assassin (Frog Two)

SCENE VALUE

The audience has witnessed the French Detective doing undercover work. "Meet Frog Two" depicts an ordinary end of the day — "off duty" — activities for the French Detective. The "cool and ruthless" assassin will be *remembered* when he arrives in N.Y.C.

SUBTEXT

The killing is a forewarning for later events in New York City: Surveillance by law enforcement may not be a secret after all.

SET-UPS

LONG-SHOT

The French Detective exits a bakery with extra-long bread. The camera follows, panning left, as the Detective turns the corner and walks into the distance.

LONG-SHOT

The French Detective approaches his building. The camera follows, panning right, as the Detective enters the hallway and stops at the mailboxes.

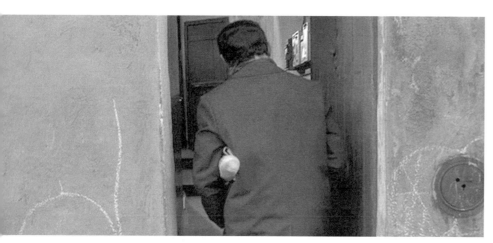

LONG-SHOT

INTERIOR HALLWAY: the Detective enters; gets mail; sees the assassin; is shot in the face and falls backward to the ground. The assassin begins to exit the building, stopping to break off the heel of the Detective's bread. The assassin throws the bread; and as he exits he takes a bite.

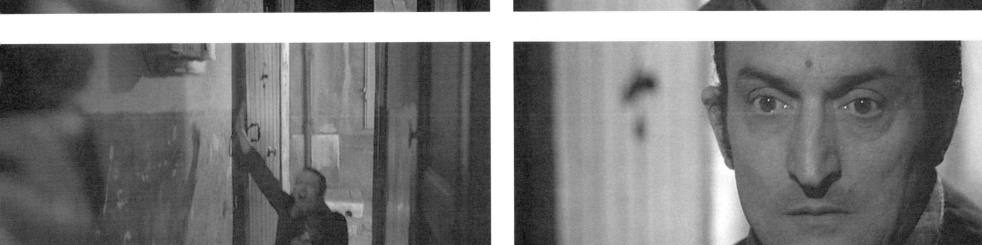

CLOSE-UP

The Detective enters the frame, gets and "checks" his mail; sees the assassin; sees the gun; looks back up to the assassin; is shot in the face, and falls backward.

CLOSE-UP

The assassin "looks" at the Detective; pulls trigger; smiles; puts gun away, and steps forward and out of frame.

CLOSE-UP

The assassin's gun. It fires, and moves out of frame.

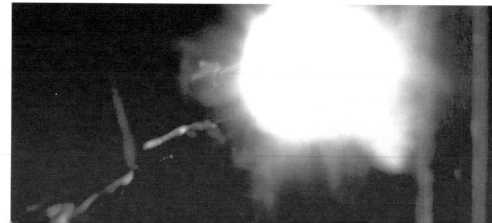

GREAT CHOICES

The *cinema verité* approach affords an authenticity. The cutting for the confrontation is determined by the eyes of the characters.

The assassin presents a slight smile.

As the assassin exits the hallway he "steals" a heel from the dead Detective's bread, throwing the rest onto the body.

The sound of a radio playing in the hallway links the "end of the day" mood to the assassin's "routine hit."

STORY

Unscrupulous Le Papet and his nephew Ugolin scheme to "steal" a neighbor's land for its access to a wealth of pure water.

SCENE

@ 0:18:01

Exterior. French Hillside. Day.

"Is the Shotgun Loaded?"

CHARACTERS

Mourners

Le Papet

Ugolin

MOURNER #1
Did you check to see if it's loaded?

MOURNER #2
I never thought of it. You can't tell with a hammerless.

MOURNER #3
I bet it's loaded with buckshot. He always kept it loaded on
account of the wild boars.

MOURNER #4
It could be dangerous. It has a hair trigger. A sudden wind
could set it off!

MOURNER #5
Maybe he set the safety?

MOURNER #6
Not him.
(mourners step to the side, out of the "line of fire")

The previous scene showed that the mourners satisfied Marius'
request that his prized shotgun be buried with him.

"Is the Shotgun Loaded?" emphasizes the "relaxed" treachery
(have they no conscience?) of Le Papet and Ugolin: An augur of
worse schemes, and consequences, to come.

The scene sets the story's foremost irony: the treachery of the
Sourbeyrans so as to successfully grow beautiful flowers.

TEXT
Contrasts the visual solemnity of the funeral procession with a
"menacing" funny side.

SUBTEXT
Since the audience knows the dirty details of Marius' death, the impulse of Le Papet and Ugolin to step to the side of the road upon finding themselves in the "line of fire," after all the other mourners have stepped aside, crafts a little "just-deserts" joke, and a foreshadowing: Even in death Marius will be an "obstacle" to Uncle and Nephew.

SET-UPS

EXTREME LONG-SHOT (HIGH-ANGLE)
Hillside: The mourners are following a horse-drawn wagon with the coffin.

LONG-SHOT (HIGH-ANGLE)
Behind funeral procession. Mourners step to the side. Le Papet and Ugolin look at each other, and step to the side.

LONG-SHOT INTO MEDIUM-SHOT
The funeral wagon approaches, and passes the camera. The mourners approach the camera and continue past exiting screen right.

MEDIUM-SHOT
From behind the mourners. They move to the sides of the road.

MEDIUM-SHOT
Le Papet and Ugolin look at each other, and step apart, and to the side.

CLOSE-UP
Rear of wagon, showing the wooden coffin's top end.

GREAT CHOICES

The edited order of the shots, and their established rhythms in action and dialogue, is so precisely integrated with the **Close-Up** of the coffin that we can experience the impending danger of a loaded shotgun joggled over the rocky roadway.

The *ambivalence* of the mourners is beautifully portrayed: Their initial demonstration of respect — marching behind the deceased — gives way to elemental self-interest.

STORY

An English-born Pakistani and his punk lover turn a begrimed East End laundrette into a luxurious laundry emporium.

SCENE

@ 0:00:01

Interior. Squatter Tenement. Day

"Squatters Out"

CHARACTERS

Johnny

Sick Friend

Pakistani Businessman

Group of Strong Arm Guys

DIALOGUE

(Johnny spots the Strong Arm Guys moving through the building)

JOHNNY
(to sick friend)
We're movin' out.

SICK FRIEND
Build a fire.

JOHNNY
It's too early in the morning.

(Strong Arm Guy #1 enters…
Johnny to Strong Arm Guy #1)
Alright…

STRONG ARM GUY #2
(to another squatter)
Get out of here. Come on.

SCENE VALUE

"Squatters Out" is the opening scene: It introduces Johnny, and immediately establishes the essential story conflict.

TEXT
Provides story-engaging curiosity about the setting, characters, actions, and substance. The scene begins a fascinating, and ongoing, battle of politics and life styles.

SUBTEXT
Reflects the tension — and *irony* — between the working class
English…

… and the (ambitious) immigrants from Pakistan.

LONG-SHOT

We can see the outside through translucent glass doors. A figure appears, and another… they move away. Suddenly the doors crash open. Strong Arm Guys push their way in.

LONG-SHOT

Apartment door. Johnny runs to the door. He opens it to "check out" the hallway. Someone runs by. Johnny closes the door. The camera pans right following him to his sick friend. Johnny helps him up, and starts gathering some possessions. A Strong Arm Guy enters frame left.

LONG-SHOT

A Strong Arm Guy pushes a squatter toward the camera, and off to the right at a staircase.

LONG-SHOT

Side of tenement. Items come through a window, followed by Johnny and his Sick Friend. The camera follows them left. They move into an **Extreme Long-Shot**. Johnny grabs some items from a clothesline, and the two head off.

MEDIUM-SHOT

Johnny is asleep sitting up. His Sick Friend is under a quilt, the mattress on the floor. Johhny awakes, and hurries off to screen right.

CLOSE-UP

Strong Arm Guy goes through apartments looking for squatters. The camera follows him from left to right. He goes back to screen left while the camera holds.

EXTREME CLOSE-UP

The frame is blocked by bodies. A Strong Arm Guy forces a squatter down the stairs. As the bodies unblock the frame we see the Pakistani Businessman in a **High-Angle Long-Shot**. He gives one last "boot" to the fleeing squatter.

GREAT CHOICES

The mysterious opening shot is smartly developed when the "blurred" figure moves away from the door.

A *beat* later, other "blurred" figures appear, and kick their way in.

STORY

Rosemary and husband Guy move into their new apartment. They are welcomed and (ultimately) "victimized" by elderly neighbors, Minnie & Roman Castevet.

SCENE

@ 1:28:06

Interior. Living Room. Day.

"Anagram"

CHARACTER

Rosemary

DIALOGUE

(using Scrabble game tiles to figure out an anagram)

ROSEMARY
Now that really makes sense! Poor Hutch…

SCENE VALUE

The audience has come to know that Rosemary's neighbors, the dear old Castevets, are not what they seem. Now Rosemary has a chance to learn the truth: Her long time, and recently deceased, friend Hutch has left her a book and a riddle: "The name is an anagram."

Rosemary gets out her Scrabble set to solve Hutch's "warning."

The final Scrabble effort exposes the true identity of Roman Castevet. Rosemary and her baby are in danger.

TEXT

Rosemary has (incorrectly) assumed that the book's title, *All of Them Witches*, is the starting point for the anagram. The solution seems out of reach. Or is it that "poor Hutch" was delusional?

SET-UPS

MEDIUM-SHOT
Rosemary enters frame right. She takes a board game from a glass cabinet. She walks away from the camera into a **Long-Shot** revealing a Scrabble game set. She spills the tiles on the floor in front of her, and begins to arrange the letters.

MEDIUM-SHOT
Rosemary examines a "leftover" tile in her hand. She begins and completes another arrangement. She stares down at the "unsuccessful solution." She begins gathering the tiles. She looks to the book, and brings it to her, opening to a dog-eared page.

MEDIUM-SHOT
Book in the background. A hand enters taking up the book, bringing it into a **Close-Up**. The book is opened to a dog-eared page; then turned to reveal a photo.

CLOSE-UP
Rosemary's POV (Point of View). The tiles spell the title of the book. A hand enters the frame and arranges, and rearranges, the tiles.

CLOSE-UP
Rosemary's face as she arranges tiles.

CLOSE-UP
Tiles in each "new" arrangement.

A hand enters and rearranges the tiles.

EXTREME CLOSE-UP
Rosemary's face as she arranges tiles.

EXTREME CLOSE-UP
Book page with the name Steven double underlined.

GREAT CHOICES

There is a brilliant use of rhythmically bold cuts. One example: The spilling of the Scrabble tiles in **Long-Shot** *cuts* to a **Close-Up** of the floor, and the (already) spelled-out book title.

Only at the beginning of Rosemary's efforts do we actually see the tiles being arranged:

A well-crafted use of Rosemary's facial and shoulder gestures, and the sound of "sliding tiles" is (nearly) all that is needed.

Take note of the lower-left corner of the frame as Rosemary brings the book toward her. On the floor is the second of her solutions, "ELF SHOT LAME WITCH," not the third and last.

It was discovered — in the editing — that utilizing Rosemary's Scrabble attempt that left a "T" in her hand in the third (and last) position, would be far better…

... than her "discouraged" words alone. *Showing* rather than *telling* that she is getting "colder" and therefore ready to gather the tiles, and "call it quits."

A perfect use of cinema: Watching the anagram reckoned and *solved!*

STORY

A tale of an aspiring writer from Virginia, and the terrible secrets of his new friends living in 1947 Brooklyn, N.Y.

SCENE

@ 2:13:24

Exterior. Nazi Concentration Camp. Night.

"Choose!"

CHARACTERS

Sophie

Son & Daughter

German Officer

German Soldiers

Prisoners

New Arrivals

OFFICER
You're so beautiful. I'd like to get you in bed. Are you a Polack?
You? Are you one of those filthy Communists?

SOPHIE
(shakes her head "no")
I'm a Pole. I was born in Cracow. I am not a Jew!
Neither are my children! They're not Jews. They are
racially pure. I'm a Christian. I'm a devout Catholic.

OFFICER
You're not a Communist?

SOPHIE
(shakes her head "no")

OFFICER
You're a believer?

SOPHIE
Yes sir. I believe in Christ!

OFFICER
So you believe in Christ the Redeemer?

SOPHIE
Yes!

OFFICER
Did He not say… "Suffer the little children… to come unto Me?"
Hmmm? You may keep one of your children.

SOPHIE
I beg your pardon?

OFFICER
You may keep one of your children. The other one must go.

SOPHIE
You mean I have to choose?

OFFICER
You're a Polack not a Yid. That gives you a privilege, a choice.

SOPHIE
I can't choose! I can't choose!

OFFICER
Be quiet!

SOPHIE
I can't choose!

OFFICER
Choose! Or I'll send them both over there! Make a choice.

SOPHIE
Don't make me choose! I can't!

OFFICER
I'll send them both over there!

SOPHIE
No!

OFFICER
Shut up! Enough… I told you to shut up! Make a choice!

SOPHIE
Don't make me choose! I can't!

OFFICER
I'll send them both over there!

SOPHIE
I can't choose!

OFFICER
(turns to soldier)
Take both children away. Move!

SOPHIE
Take my little girl! Take my baby!
(The soldier walks off carrying the screaming daughter.)

Take my little girl…

SCENE VALUE

Early in the film we "noted" numbers tattooed on Sophie's arm: She is a concentration camp survivor. This scene reveals the awful secret so softly stated in the title.

TEXT
Beginning with a flirtatious introduction, the Officer proceeds with malevolently calm "logic," incorporating political and religious conversation, interspersed with mocking nods of his head, all adding up to devastating apprehension.

... in the attractive elegance of the German Officer...

... we find *unfathomable evil.*

EXTREME LONG-SHOT
The camera moves right, past concentration camp arrivals. Some prisoners help soldiers keep people in line. The camera "finds" Sophie and her children. An Officer approaches and stops in front of Sophie.

EXTREME LONG-SHOT
The camera pans left following a "wandering" prisoner along the tracks, past empty baby carriages. We see "gaps" in the lines of the new arrivals.

LONG-SHOT
Line of arrivals showing Sophie and her children.

LONG-SHOT
Officer orders a soldier to take Sophie's children. Sophie makes her choice! Soldier carries the daughter away.

MEDIUM LONG-SHOT
Officer enters frame right walking away from Sophie. We "stay" on his back as he pauses, then turns to look at Sophie. He walks back to her.

MEDIUM-SHOT
Sophie's son staying close to his mother. A soldier grabs him; then lets go of him.

MEDIUM-SHOT
Sophie holding daughter. Officer approaches and stops. Shot continues over Officer's left shoulder.

MEDIUM-SHOT
Over Officer's left shoulder. He turns, and calls soldier. A soldier hurries over, and begins to take both children. Sophie makes her choice and the soldier takes the daughter.

MEDIUM-SHOT
Daughter in Sophie's arms. Soldier enters the frame and takes the daughter.

MEDIUM CLOSE-UP
Sophie with her daughter in her arms.

CLOSE-UP
Officer enters frame left. Engages Sophie, and exits frame right.

CLOSE-UP
Sophie and daughter.

CLOSE-UP
Full face view of Sophie and daughter looking to Officer who has walked away.

CLOSE-UP

From behind Sophie. The Officer "returns" entering frame right.

CLOSE-UP

Son in front of Sophie. Soldier's hands grab him, then leave him.

CLOSE-UP

Sophie over Officer's left shoulder.

CLOSE-UP

The Soldier blocks the frame, then moves to screen left revealing Sophie; she turns and faces the camera. She watches her daughter carried away.

GREAT CHOICES

The flirtatiousness of the Officer suggests the possibility of "protection" for Sophie and her children.

The Officer walks away, but with dreadful *irony*, Sophie "encourages" him back to her. Take note of the change in the camera axis — on Sophie and her Daughter's *second* **Close-Up** — to better "represent" the "look back" of the Officer. And! Look at the absolute horror on the face of the Daughter!

Note the "mocking" head nods of the Officer when he reacts to Sophie's responses. This along with the "understated" tone — and unexpected quiet — makes the outcome all the more horrifying.

As the Daughter is carried off, Sophie's mouth opens to scream; but she emits *not* a sound:

The "suffering" cries of her Daughter "play" across Sophie's face.

STORY

Joe Turner, a CIA researcher working out of a Manhattan "front organization," returns with take-out lunch orders for his colleagues and finds that they've all been murdered. He flees the building, and, uncertain of whom he can trust, goes into hiding.

SCENE

@ 0:11:34

Exterior/Interior. NYC Streets/Office. Day.

"Out to Lunch"

CHARACTERS

Joubert

Driver

Joe Turner

"Mailman"

"Messenger"

Mrs. Russell (Receptionist)

Dr. Lappe

"Sarge"

SCENE VALUE

"Out to Lunch" is the scene that sets the central plot in motion. It does a good deal more than provide gripping movie suspense: It creates a driving curiosity for the audience — as well as for Joe Turner. Neither Turner, nor the audience, knows the "why" of "what" takes place; and not (really) the "who" either.

SET-UPS

EXTERIOR SHOTS

LONG-SHOT
Quiet Manhattan street, following a heavy downpour.

LONG-SHOT
Street corner. Man in rain poncho ("Messenger") comes around the corner. The camera pans right, well ahead of "Messenger," and holds on the building of attention: American Literary Historical Society.

LONG-SHOT
Man in rain poncho walking toward camera; "Mailman" enters frame right walking toward "Messenger."

LONG-SHOT
Turner exits luncheonette with take-out for the "Society" staff.

MEDIUM LONG-SHOT
Joubert looks to the left (toward mailman); looks to right (toward "poncho-man"); and watches the two approaching the building of attention.

MEDIUM-SHOT
Car with "associate" leaves curb. Wet pavement reflects Joubert. Camera tilts upward as he moves to foreground, and out of frame left, leaving a blurred background.

MEDIUM CLOSE-UP
Mailman walks to screen left "in" a long focal length lens shot.

CLOSE-UP
Profile of Joubert. He turns to look to far corner. Rack focus reveals mailman in **Long-Shot** coming around the corner walking to screen left.

INTERIOR SHOTS

LONG-SHOT
Mrs. Russell at her desk is typing. She looks down at the sound of the front door's "buzz." She opens the desk drawer and "buzzes" back, unlocking the front door. The camera pans left, and dollies in to a **Close-Up** of the entering Mailman.

LONG-SHOT
"Society's" guard comes from a back room; he sees the "danger" and the camera follows him right. He is shot and falls.

LONG-SHOT (LOOKING UP)

Dr. Lappe comes down the stairs. Gunshots blast away at him. Smoke and bullet holes fill the stairway.

MEDIUM LONG-SHOT

Dr. Lappe falls down the stairs, coming to rest in the foreground.

MEDIUM CLOSE-UP

Mrs. Russell is typing; looks down (at "doorbell" cue); reaches back, opens the desk drawer to "buzz in" the "Mailman."

MEDIUM-SHOT

Mrs. Russell at her desk, typing. Responds to "doorbell": Looks down, turns to ring the desk drawer "buzzer." Gunshots hurl her backward, toppling her in her chair; and filling the wall with bullet holes.

MEDIUM CLOSE-UP (POV)

Mrs. Russell's POV sees Mailman on security monitor below her desk.

MEDIUM CLOSE-UP

The Mailman and "Poncho-Man" look up toward the stairway, and open fire.

CLOSE-UP

Automatic rifle barrel firing. It is Poncho-Man's weapon.

CLOSE-UP

Joubert's POV of the spinning book rack. Bullet holes are evident. His hand lifts the top revealing a surveillance VCR. He removes the tape.

CLOSE-UP

Joubert enters. Looks about. Camera dollies back with him — into a **Medium Shot** — to the spinning book rack. Joubert stops the spinning, and lifts the top off of the rack. He puts it down, and pulls the security video tape from inside.

GREAT CHOICES

Here is an excellent juxtaposition of images "playing" the gathering hit team as it makes its way to the American Literary Historical Society: Joubert "orchestrates" the cuts, with POV shots from across the street, which introduce "Mailman" and "Messenger." Take note of the effective use of *rack-focus*.

As a car driven by another "team" member pulls away from the curb, Joubert crosses the street: Beginning with his reflection in the wet street to his face filling the frame.

After "Mailman" enters, there is a cut to Mrs. Russell:

It is *then* that a burst of gunfire "hits" our ears; pitilessly killing Mrs. Russell.

A brilliant use of *irony*: If not for the rain, Joe would not have exited through the basement on his way to the luncheonette, and been spared the fate of his colleagues.

Dramatic Irony: The audience knows — the "Society's" staff does not — that an imminent peril exists.

The edited order creates an ever-greater sense of Joubert as the icy professional: He doesn't look up upon hearing Dr. Lappe's voice as he descends the stairs, but only after Dr. Lappe is shot.

STORY

Cesira and her daughter Rosetta flee Rome and the horrors of World War II Allied bombing. They survive the difficult journey to Cesira's native mountain village.

SCENE

@ 1:17:21

Interior. Church. Day.

"Rape"

CHARACTERS

Cesira

Rosetta

Moroccan Soldiers

SCENE VALUE

"Rape" is a scene of multiple contrasts and ironies: The war in Italy is virtually over; Cesira and Rosetta are returning home. They seek shelter in an extensively damaged church, and prepare for sleep. A group of Moroccan soldiers finds them.

SUBTEXT

Beyond themes about the madness and malice of war is the bond, and *responsibility*, of Cesira — a single mother — to Rosetta; and especially here, in a Catholic church:

The Church is a sanctuary, and so an apparently good choice as a place to rest. The soldiers are Moroccan, and more than likely Muslim.

Cesira exhibits no personal fear, but is horrified for her daughter. Rosetta is a virgin.

EXTREME LONG-SHOT
Mother and Rosetta enter the church. Mother prepares benches for napping. Rosetta approaches the altar, crosses herself, and curtseys. She walks back toward the benches, and settles to nap. Mother sets herself on another bench. Soldiers appear in the doorway, and then run off. Mother awakens Rosetta, and they try to leave the church. A group of soldiers rush into the church, and grab Mother and Rosetta. The women break free, and run; the soldiers go after them.

LONG-SHOT
Mother tries to sleep. She hears something, sits up, and goes to wake Rosetta. The camera moves back. Soldiers rush in. The women run toward the altar. Mother breaks free, and runs toward the camera; it pans right following the Mother and soldiers rushing away. The soldiers leap over a suddenly stopping and bending mother. She picks up a large stone. Rosetta comes running past Mother, who throws the stone at the soldiers, and runs with her daughter toward the camera. The camera follows now panning left into the main chapel.

LONG-SHOT
Mother cleans a bench for herself, and lies upon it. The camera tilts downward, as shadows of soldiers are cast across the lighted doorway.

LONG-SHOT
Mother is chased by soldiers into an aisle-way to the right of the chapel. Soldiers pursue her. She stops, and bends. Soldiers leap over her. Mother picks up a stone, and throws it as Rosetta hurries from the background. Mother and Rosetta hurry away with the soldiers after them.

LONG-SHOT
Rosetta's POV. Looking up to the open church roof. Insects fly and buzz about.

LONG-SHOT
Mother's POV. Rosetta on the ground, surrounded and held by soldiers.

MEDIUM LONG-SHOT
Soldiers stand at the church doorway reacting to their comrade's pursuit of Mother and Rosetta.

MEDIUM LONG-SHOT
Mother clears a bench for Rosetta, and helps "tuck" her in, using a sweater to fashion a pillow.

MEDIUM LONG-SHOT
Mother is thrown to the ground, and turns toward the camera to "find" Rosetta. A soldier covers her mouth, and turns her head to him. Mother bites his hand, and the soldier takes revenge by hitting her head on the ground.

MEDIUM-SHOT
Mother and Rosetta enter the church. Rosetta crosses herself, and curtseys. The camera follows with a pan to the right into a **Long-Shot**. Mother begins to "arrange" and clean benches for napping. Rosetta walks toward the church altar.

MEDIUM CLOSE-UP
Rosetta places her head on the pillow. She looks up to the opened roof, and then settles to sleep.

MEDIUM CLOSE-UP
Rosetta with a bloodied lip. Camera zooms-in to a **Close-Up** of her face.

CLOSE-UP
Mother thrown to the ground. Soldiers hold and battle her. Mother turns to "find" Rosetta. A soldier's hand covers her mouth. Mother bites the hand. The hand struggles free, and the soldier takes revenge, repeatedly slamming mother's head on the ground, knocking her unconscious.

GREAT CHOICES

Great storytelling — *storyshowing* — by ever increasing tension: Before falling to sleep, Rosetta looks up and *through* the damaged roof. We see (in Rosetta's POV), and we hear, the "buzzing/humming" of swarming insects.

The elongated shadows cast upon the floor in the opened doorway of the church not only foreshadow the women's danger, but hint at a previous scene when a company of Moroccan soldiers passed Cesira and Rosetta on the road.

There is an extensive use of Dramatic Irony. The *audience* sees the soldiers' shadows; *neither woman* does.

But! Later the audience *and* Cesira see the smiling Moroccan soldier peering in: The soldier appears in the background beyond the sleeping Rosetta. Rosetta is "innocent"… *not knowing!*

DELIGHTS

STORY

Colonel Sergei Kotov, a hero of the Russian Revolution, is a target of "political paranoia" during the Stalinist purges of the mid-1930s.

CHARACTERS

Colonel Kotov

Nadya (his daughter)

SCENE

@ 1:49:05

Interior. Colonel Kotov's Home Office. Day.

"Platypus"

NADYA
Papa! Papa! There you are… Why is your cup here? Have you been drinking?

KOTOV
Me?

NADYA
Yes.

KOTOV
(nods "yes")

NADYA
And you've eaten nothing?

KOTOV
No.

NADYA
Where are you off to? Are you leaving?

KOTOV
The car's here… I'm going to Moscow. I'm getting ready.

NADYA
And your car?

KOTOV
It'll come tomorrow at nine o'clock. I have an appointment at…
(holds up eight fingers)

NADYA
(counts fingers)
Eight!

KOTOV
Eight! Very good….

NADYA
Come on. Hurry up. Uncle Mitya said that I could drive a little. As far as the bend… Daddy hurry… come on! Daddy do you remember Uncle Mitya's story? They all had funny names. Well do you know if I had been in the story what my name would have been?

KOTOV
What?

NADYA
Yadan.

KOTOV
Yadan? What does that mean?

NADYA
It's Nadya spelled backwards. Hurry up.

KOTOV
You know tomorrow… we can't go to the zoo. I have to work.
Don't be angry with me.

NADYA
We'll go another time.

KOTOV
Do the platypus for me. Oh! He's so pretty.

NADYA
Can you play this game?

KOTOV
What game?

NADYA
Look… You plug your ears and you go "OOOH."

KOTOV
What?

NADYA
Like this… Look! "OOOH."

KOTOV
Really?

NADYA
Yes. Three, four…

KOTOV & NADYA
"OOOOOOH…."

NADYA
(runs out of breath)
I'm little. I get two chances. "OOOH…."

(runs out of breath again)
Three times. I get to go three times because I'm little. Three,
four…"OOOH…."

(runs out of breath a third time. Stares in awe at the still
"OOOHing" Kotov)
How about that!!!

SCENE VALUE

Papa and Nadya's "delightful teasing" and "game playing" — they deeply adore each other — launches a sinister scene ahead.

TEXT

The reference to "Uncle" Mitya, his story, and Nadya's happy feelings about him, are forcefully contrasted by "Uncle" Mitya's true identity and purpose.

SUBTEXT

Note the interesting "role reversal" moments: Nadya "scolds" her father for drinking, helps him dress, and "teaches" him a game he's never played. And yet, Nadya is quick to claim a child's rules exemption at shortness of breath!

The camera move-in to the photo of a smiling Kotov and Stalin connects back to the endearing term, "Uncle" for Mitya: The despot Stalin was often affectionately called "Uncle."

Nadya's innocence is maintained: Papa "protects" her from the truth about his drinking and leaving.

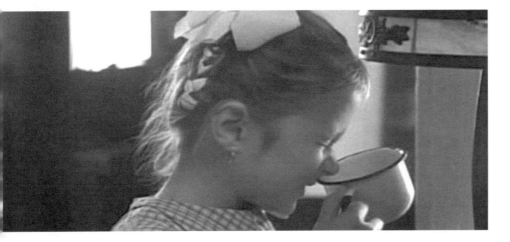

SET-UPS

LONG-SHOT
Nadya enters her father's office. She moves into **Close-Up**: We realize that Nadya was initially reflected in a mirror…

… she lifts her father's enamel cup to her nose, and "makes a face" at the odor of strong alcohol.

She "forgives" Father's drinking with a silly sound, and grimace; then walks to him exiting the frame.

MEDIUM LONG-SHOT

Kotov from behind Nadya. They "play" count time; Nadya exits screen left; reappears with her father's tunic; helps him dress; plays "Platypus", and then the "Oooh" game, while a very slow move-in brings us to a **Close-Up**.

MEDIUM-SHOT

Nadya from over Kotov's left shoulder. They "play" count time; Nadya hurries to a chair in the background to get her father's tunic; returns to the foreground to help him dress; plays "Platypus", and then the "Oooh" game. The camera racks focus to "follow" her to the background, and again into the foreground; then proceeds with a very slow move-in to **Close-Up.**

MEDIUM-SHOT

A framed photo of Kotov with Joseph Stalin sits on a desk. The camera slowly moves-in to hold on a **Close-Up**.

Two of the set-ups provide a wide array of compositions with (very) slow move-ins. The moves are so subtle and well motivated by the text, subtext, and actions that we hardly notice that the changing compositions are derived from a continuous camera run. And! Don't forget the two "rack focus" moments of the shot from over Kotov's left shoulder. Beautifully simple (not easy) production!

Nadya's helping Papa to dress, demonstrates — along with her "scolding" him for drinking on an empty stomach — care-taking strengths that "promise" a hopeful future in the face of her family's ruin.

The Cut Away/Insert of the photo with Stalin, and the haunting music played on wind instruments, "mirrors" the game of "OOOH" while it "indicates" Papa's heroic past, and the peril he knows awaits him.

The "silliness" between Papa and Nadya generates great affection, and contrasts the advancing threat — without expository dialogue.

Take note of the "beats" (pause) between Kotov's "*No*" and Nadya's "*Where are you off to?*" A rhythmically effective construction of a dramatic transition: change in inflection; changing topic.

Children of a Lesser God: 1986 | 119 minutes | United States | Randa Haines

STORY

James Leeds is a new teacher at a school for the hearing-impaired. He meets, and falls in love with, Sarah, a graduate of the school now working as a staff member, unable to face the outside world.

CHARACTERS

James

Students

SCENE

@ 0:05:43

Interior. Classroom. Day.

"Just Testing"

MALE STUDENT
Are we being punished?

JAMES
(sitting at his desk gazing off into space; tipping from his chair)

(the students don't know what to make of James)

JAMES
(leaps to his feet speaking & signing)
Hi! I'm James Leeds and my signing is rusty.

So! How many of you can read lips? No one?!

Class dismissed!

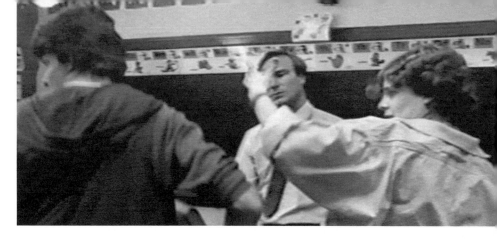

(students hurry to leave)
No, no, no, no, no, no, no, no… just testing. Sit down!

(to student in the last desk)
You mind closing your notebook?

(closing the notebook for the student)
Thank you.

SCENE VALUE

We see James for the first time with his new students. His teaching approach is vibrant, enjoyable, and caring: The scene sets James apart at the school — leading to a few obstacles — and establishes his relationship to the class.

TEXT

The opening line, "Are we being punished?" raises the likelihood that rigid discipline is a common approach to teaching.

SUBTEXT

By scene's end the mood has convinced the audience that James and his students have quickly built a "winning" relationship. This furnishes an essential contrast to James' later efforts with Sarah.

SET-UPS

LONG-SHOT

Profile along the line of the students. One student stands to see the fallen James.

LONG-SHOT

From behind students. James sits at his desk gazing off to nowhere. He tilts to screen right, falls to the floor, gets up, and comes to the front of his desk, sits, and introduces himself. The students hurry to leave, and James stops them; the camera then pans left following James to the student at the last desk.

LONG-SHOT

From slightly behind James. He comes around the desk and sits. The students begin to leave and he stops them.

MEDIUM LONG-SHOT

James sits at his desk gazing off. He slowly tilts to screen right, falls on the floor. He gets up and sits on the front of his desk. He dismisses the class; then stops them.

MEDIUM-SHOT

Dolly right past the students. The last student stops writing and looks up.

MEDIUM-SHOT

Two students react to James' silent gazing.

CLOSE-UP

James sits on the front of his desk. He dismisses the class, and then stops them.

CLOSE-UP

Female Student.

CLOSE-UP

Male Student.

GREAT CHOICES

The scene opens with the camera moving past the line of students. The sound of an electric razor accompanies the camera move.

We get to a student who is shaving with the electric razor. The sound doesn't disrupt the class: This is a school for the hearing-impaired.

The last student looks up and toward the front of the classroom; his "focus" motivates the cut to James at his desk, gazing off into space. The humor is not one of sarcasm, nor ridicule, but rather affectionate play. An effective divulging of the characters and classroom with limited, yet smart, coverage.

STORY

Alfred Redl begins his military career as a boy cadet,
and ends as Chief of Military Intelligence for the Austro-Hungarian Army.

SCENE

@ 0:10:57

Interior. Kubyni Estate Living Room. Day.

"Spigot"

CHARACTERS

Alfred

Kristof Kubyni

Katalin (Kristof's Sister)

Grandmother

Grandfather

Butler

Maids

DIALOGUE

*(During Katalin's "concert" Alfred takes
Grandfather's cup for a refill)*

ALFRED
(unable to stop the flow of coffee)
Can someone help me?

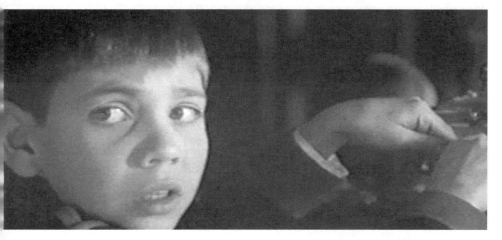

SCENE VALUE

"Spigot" is part of a multi-scene sequence. Alfred — from a family of modest stature — has befriended Kristof Kubyni at the cadet academy. Kristof has invited him to his grandparent's elegant estate. Alfred has studied the Kubynis' etiquette. Dutifully on his best behavior, Redl offers to refill the grandfather's coffee cup: The spigot won't shut, wetting the floor and oriental rug.

The scene ends with the affectionate start of a lifetime friendship between Alfred and Katalin.

SUBTEXT

No matter his diligence, dedication, and intelligence, Alfred Redl will never *completely* "fit in" to the Hapsburg aristocracy.

SET-UPS

EXTREME LONG-SHOT
Alfred and grandparents watch Kristof and Katalin at the piano.

EXTREME LONG-SHOT
Alfred at the coffee urn.

EXTREME LONG-SHOT
Butler enters the living room. The camera pans right following him to the urn, then holds as two maids approach, and begin the clean-up. A third maid enters frame left. The camera follows the action: tilting down, and panning left.

LONG-SHOT
Alfred, Kristof, Katalin, and Grandparents sit around a small table. Katalin pours a cup of coffee; and then delicately and intentionally tips the cup, spilling all of the coffee onto her white gown.

MEDIUM LONG-SHOT
Grandmother "listens" to the music; she turns responding to Alfred, and rings her servant's bell.

MEDIUM-SHOT

Slightly to the front of the piano. Kristof turns the music pages for Katalin.

MEDIUM CLOSE-UP

Alfred in the foreground, grandfather in the background. Rack-focus from Alfred to Grandfather as Alfred notices the grandfather's cup is empty. Alfred gets up and takes the cup. The grandfather pats his back in a "thank you." The camera follows panning right, into a **Medium Long-Shot** as Alfred stops at a fireplace mantle. Alfred refills the grandfather's cup from a silver urn, but he can't stop the flow of coffee.

MEDIUM CLOSE-UP

From behind Katalin. She looks back (to Alfred). She smiles, and then turns to the keyboard.

CLOSE-UP

Alfred jiggling the spigot and urn. He looks to the grandparents, back to the urn, and back to the grandparents.

CLOSE-UP

High-Angle (Alfred's POV) on Maid.

CLOSE-UP

Low-Angle (Maid's POV), Alfred embarrassed.

CLOSE-UP

Alfred smiles to Katalin after she spills coffee in her lap.

EXTREME CLOSE-UP

Alfred's hand "battling" the coffee urn spigot.

GREAT CHOICES

Foremost: The well-crafted *set-ups* that follow the *emotion* in the actions around the room. Especially take note of the **Medium Close-Up** from behind Katalin as Alfred "battles" the spigot.

There is a "break" in the time structure between the "clean-up" and Katalin's purposely soiling her gown: When the maid smiles sympathetically, Alfred feels no less shame. But! Katalin's " accident," and the grandmother's shock, earn a relieved and thankful smile.

The terrible moments at the coffee urn *before* Alfred's call for help simultaneously captivates the audience in dismay and enchantment.

Listen to the outstanding use of the piano music: for the overall setting; Kristof and Katalin's relationship, and to "carry" Alfred to the mantle and urn.

STORY

One year — 1907 — in the life of the Ekdahl family.

SCENE

@ 0:24:28

Interior. Ekdahl Home. Night.

"Uncle Carl's Fireworks"

CHARACTERS

Uncle Carl

Fanny

Alexander

Cousins

Father

UNCLE CARL
Children come! Uncle Carl is going to treat you to fireworks!

(the children follow Uncle Carl past Father...)

(… to a grand staircase)
Stay here…

(Uncle Carl runs up and down the stairs…)

(… then up again, and he lets a fart)
Number one.

(Uncle Carl hurries down the stairs)
Now comes number two.
(he lets another fart)

Now the third. Bring the candles.

(Uncle Carl "drops his pants" and
"blows" out the candles)

A Christmas celebration of enchantment: The scene is part of a child's memory sequence. The extended family holiday festivities are soon contrasted by the unexpected death of Father. "Uncle Carl's Fireworks" allows the audience a glimpse of Father as the children and Uncle Carl pass him on the way to the stairs. Father does not look well.

SUBTEXT
Here is a fairy-tale: Uncle Carl, Pied Piper-like, "steals" the children. An imminent "consequence" is the death of Father, and Alexander's terror — and revulsion.

SET-UPS

EXTREME LONG-SHOT
Uncle Carl and the children move from the far background toward and past the camera. The camera pans right stopping on a **Close-Up** of Father. He is feeling ill.

LONG-SHOT
The camera follows Uncle Carl and the children down a staircase. The camera holds on a **Medium-Shot** of the children. Alexander moves into a **Close-Up** to take hold of the candelabra.

MEDIUM-SHOT
Uncle Carl sits with his cigar. In the background — in soft focus — the children "appear" somersaulting into the room. Uncle Carl gets up, moving into the background **Long-Shot** as the camera racks focus. Unlce Carl picks up a candelabra, and they all exit frame right.

MEDIUM-SHOT into a **Long-Shot** as the camera follows Uncle Carl down the next flight, panning left. He sits and removes his boots and pants. The camera follows as he runs up and down the stairs. As he returns up the stairs the camera zooms in to meet his face in an **Extreme Close-Up**. He pauses and farts. He then proceeds down the stairs, the camera following. He pauses and farts. He starts up the stairs more slowly, pulling down the "rear" flap of his underwear. He stops in a Low-Angle **Medium-Shot**. Uncle Carl turns his back to the children. The children, led by Alexander with the candelabra, come up behind him.

MEDIUM-SHOT
The children come close to the banister railing. They sit or crouch to watch Uncle Carl.

MEDIUM-SHOT
Uncle Carl arrives in screen left. Alexander, with the candelabra, leads the children in a kneeling/crouching action to a position behind the turning Uncle Carl. Uncle Carl farts again, blowing out the candles. (The frame "pops" to black.)

GREAT CHOICES

The scene's portrayal of childhood reminiscence is established with compositions depicting the POV of the children.

The "stop and hold" on the Father is an ill-omened clue of dramatic irony.

The set-ups are enhanced by *foreground to background*, and *background to foreground* movement of the characters: Along with the well-timed and motivated camera moves, they establish a rich spatial environment.

Uncle Carl's quick dashes up and down the staircase build to the "explosive" ending.

The Four Hundred Blows: 1959 | 97 minutes | France | François Truffaut

STORY

Twelve-year-old Antoine tries to find his way in a world of enigmatic adults.

SCENE

@ 0:21:13

Interior. Amusement Park Ride. Day.

"Spinning"

CHARACTERS

Antoine

Friend

Other Riders

Spectators

Ride Operator

Antoine and his friend *continue* to skip school: "Spinning" is part of a montage of a "day on the town." This delightful adventure leads to Antoine's catching sight of his mother in the arms of "another" man. Antoine and his mother — she sees him as well; he's "not in school" — hold secrets neither wants revealed to Antoine's father. This provokes Antoine's ever-mounting delinquencies.

SUBTEXT

What is effectively a "freedom-filled" fun ride echoes Antoine's "swirlingly" perplexing world.

SET-UPS

LONG-SHOT

High-Angle into an amusement park centrifugal wheel ride. Antoine and other riders enter.

The camera moves upward as the ride begins; holds; then moves down as the ride slows and stops.

Antoine, and fellow riders, exit.

LONG-SHOT

The camera looks up at the Spectators; moves in and holds on a **Medium Long-Shot**. The Spectators "spin" faster and faster.

The **Shot** is turned over, representing the POV of Antoine when he is spinning upside-down.

MEDIUM-SHOT
Antoine as the ride begins, and accelerates.

As the ride increases speed he is "lifted" from the floor... the camera tilts down to his shoes, then tilts back up to follow Antoine's maneuvers. He struggles to turn himself upside down, rights himself, and "drops" back to the floor as the ride slows to a stop.

GREAT CHOICES

The *intercutting* — the back and forth and back and forth — of selected moments from the three set-ups, along with the sound of the spinning machinery and the "whooping" of riders and spectators, makes this a "great ride" for the audience.

An uninhibited production style brings a "Spinning" smile to Antoine… and us!

Positioning this scene *last* in the montage (sequence) of Antoine's "Day on the Town" generates a contrasting twist to Antoine's catching sight of his mother with her "companion": A joyful "break" returns him to "nasty" realities!

Kolya: 1996 | 112 minutes | Czechoslovakia | Jan Sverak

STORY

Frantisek, a middle-aged classical musician, trying to "make ends meet" in 1988 Prague, agrees to marry a Russian émigré for a large sum of money. The woman "disappears," leaving him to care for her five-year old son, while he fends off the investigating authorities.

SCENE

@ 0:01:03

Interior. Chapel. Day.

"Naughty Bow"

CHARACTERS

Frantisek

Singer

Musicians

Mourners

*(Frantisek uses his bow to "sneak" up
and under the singer's dress)*

SINGER
(hitting Franta with the sheet music)
Pig! Grow up, can't you?

MUSICIAN 1
Coffee anyone? Franta?

FRANTISEK
No! I'm in a hurry.

MUSICIAN 2
Another job? You must be rolling in it!

This is our introduction to Frantisek (Franta).

A teapot whistle "signals" his adroitness with the bow…

… and his hands!

TEXT
Relates Frantisek's freelance status. And! We will soon learn that notwithstanding Musician 2's comment "You must be rolling in it," Frantisek is in a financial quandary, which leads to his taking action that is central to the plot of the story.

SUBTEXT
Frantisek, a cellist, is a free spirit with a keen eye for the ladies.

"Naughty Bow" demonstrates Franta's "daring" nonconformity in Soviet-dominated Czechoslovakia:

His "ass grab" of the singer during the funeral service turns heads… and illuminates Franta's personal predicament — he's been fired by the prestigious, and no doubt unadventurous, Czech Symphony Orchestra. This prompts the plot of the film, and sets the obstacles and consequences that unfold.

SET-UPS

LONG-SHOT
Tilt down past chapel windows to the musicians.

LONG-SHOT
From the front of the chapel. Mourners at a funeral service. They react to a startled screech. They look back and up to the balcony.

LONG-SHOT
From over the Singer's right shoulder looking down from the balcony to the chapel.

MEDIUM LONG-SHOT
From behind Frantisek. He turns to the kettle. The camera follows him up. With his bow he slaps the whistling cap off the kettle. The Singer takes her place along the balcony rail. She sings the Lord's Prayer. Frantisek plays his bow up to the Singer's skirt, lifting it. At the hymn's conclusion the Singer hits Frantisek on the head with the music book. She exits.

MEDIUM-SHOT

The Singer at the balcony rail.

MEDIUM-SHOT

Frantisek's hand reaching out and "goosing" the singer.

MEDIUM-SHOT

Frantisek. Pan right and rack focus to the Singer.

CLOSE-UP

Musicians watching, then smiling at Frantisek's "playfulness."

CLOSE-UP

Cello. The camera tilts up to Frantisek.

CLOSE-UP

Over Singer's right shoulder. Rack focus, pan right, and tilt down to chapel below.

CLOSE-UP

The singer's feet take their position at the balcony rail as the kettle cap rolls along the floor.

EXTREME CLOSE-UP

Tapping foot. The camera racks focus to a beer bottle on the floor, and moves up to a violin.

EXTREME CLOSE-UP

Kettle. Steam bursts from the whistling cap.

EXTREME CLOSE-UP

The back of the Singer's legs. The bow enters the frame and "plays" the edge of her skirt, and lifts it.

GREAT CHOICES

A delightful juxtaposition of funereal solemnity…

… and boisterous "fun."

A beautiful example of the camera gracefully exploring the setting.

STORY

Seven-year-old Joey believes that he's killed his older brother Lennie, and "escapes" to Coney Island, Brooklyn.

SCENE

@ 0:43:37

Exterior. Coney Island Beach. Day.

"That's a Nice Boy"

CHARACTERS

Joey

Mother

Baby

Coney Island Beach Goers

DIALOGUE

MOTHER
(to Baby)
Come on, drink the water. Stop wiggling…
come on… Baby… Alright!

(Joey bumps the Mother, causing the water to spill)

Oh! Sonny, look what you did? Now I have to go all the way back
to the fountain for some more.

JOEY
I'll get it lady!

MOTHER
That's a nice boy! It'll only take you a few minutes.

JOEY
Watch my bottles, please?

MOTHER
Put them here….

*(Joey puts down his two bottles. Mother gives
Joey a paper cup. Joey walks off)*

(to Baby)
Oh, baby….

SCENE VALUE

Joey's learned that a little money can be made by collecting and redeeming discarded soda bottles. He has just begun — gathering but two — when he "bumps" into Mother and Baby.

TEXT
Mother's "That's a nice boy. It'll only take a few minutes" sets up Joey's moment of ambivalence:

SUBTEXT
His decent conscience leads to an attempt to make up for the *spilled water*; but given the great difficulty, and last-second "accident," Joey abandons his deposit bottles rather than offer another apology, or try the public fountain again. Is he *thinking* that the bottles (left with the mother) will "pay" for disappointing her?

We can all identify with Joey's ambivalence. It's why the scene makes us (nervously) chuckle.

LONG-SHOT
Joey at edge of crowd at drinking fountain.

LONG-SHOT
Joey winding his way past beach goers, into a **Close-Up** past the camera. Joey, passing beach goers, walks into the foreground. Joey falls — spilling the water.

He looks ahead (toward the waiting Mother and Baby), then turns and crawls away.

LONG-SHOT

Joey's POV of Mother and Baby awaiting his return.

MEDIUM-SHOT
Mother and Baby; as Joey approaches, he spills the water.

The camera repositions to the right as Joey leaves his bottles and exits.

MEDIUM-SHOT(S)
From behind gathered bathers at water fountain.

CLOSE-UP
Baby in Mother's arms.

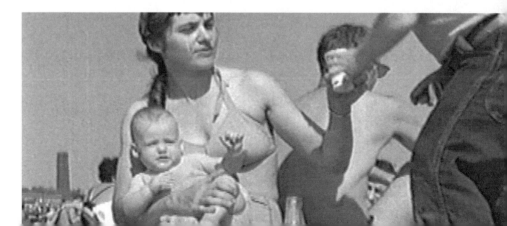

GREAT CHOICES

The film's inventive use of *cinema verité* inspired European directors, including François Truffaut.

Good storytelling connections: Joey's newly discovered "soda bottle money-making" is cut short by a new obstacle, which leads to a moral dilemma.

The audience never sees the fountain: Joey disappears into the crowd, and finally reappears. And! He's soaked! We can pretty well imagine the battle for water.

The music bonds Joey to his brother: Lennie's *harmonica* was given to Joey just before he took flight to Coney Island.

STORY

New Year's celebrations "require" a decorative gold fish. Little Razieh is not happy with her "skinny fish"; she wants one of the beautiful fantail goldfish she's seen in the marketplace.

SCENE

@ 0:17:24

Exterior. Courtyard. Day.

"One Hundred for a Fish?"

CHARACTERS

Razieh

Ali (Brother)

Mother

ALI
Mum?

MOTHER
What now? I've already said no!

ALI
Let me tell you just one thing.

MOTHER
I know what you're going to say, and I've had enough of it.

ALI
Just a second… promise you won't get angry! Just a second.

MOTHER
Do as you're told.

ALI
If you don't agree I won't ask anymore.

MOTHER
All right.

ALI
Come closer!

MOTHER
Just say it.

ALI
I want to whisper it to you.

MOTHER
Come on, say it!

(Ali goes inside and whispers to "Mum")
Okay. Get my bag.

(Ali hurries outside to get the bag)

RAZIEH
So?

ALI
Okay! But don't forget your promise.

RAZIEH
I told you it's yours.

ALI
Stay over there, she mustn't see you.
(Ali hurries back inside)

MOTHER
Check how much money is left.

ALI
Two twenties.

MOTHER
What about the small pocket?

ALI
A five-hundred note.

MOTHER
How much was the goldfish?

RAZIEH
One hundred!

MOTHER
One hundred for a fish?

RAZIEH
The shopkeeper said they all cost one hundred.
Without the bowl.

MOTHER
Take the five-hundred note and go get one for her.

(Ali hurries outside)

ALI
So is the balloon mine?

RAZIEH
Yes it is!

(Razieh hurries off with an empty bowl
and the five-hundred note)

ALI
Promise?!

RAZIEH
Yes, take it.

MOTHER
You aren't allowed to go…

RAZIEH
I'll be back soon.

SCENE VALUE

This scene thrusts Razieh on a long, and often frustrating, adventure to acquire her beautiful fish.

SUBTEXT

While some of the themes may be particular to Iranian culture, many more seem universal: Brother and sister "ganging up" on Mother to persuade; brother Ali is the emissary to Mother — is it because he's older, or male?

SET-UPS

LONG-SHOT
Razieh's POV of Ali trying to persuade "Mum" to listen.

MEDIUM LONG-SHOT
Ali whispers to Mother (the reasons to say "yes") as he follows Mother around the living room while she vacuums. The camera follows left as Ali stops to put on his shoes and then hurries to Razieh.

MEDIUM-SHOT
Ali returns with Mother's bag... and gets money for Razieh.

MEDIUM-SHOT
Razieh gets the money from Ali and runs off into **Long-Shot.**

MEDIUM CLOSE-UP
Razieh, in a crouch, watches Ali "plead" his case to "Mum."

MEDIUM CLOSE-UP
Razieh watches. She runs into a **Long-Shot** to "greet" Ali getting the Mother's bag. She returns to her original place to watch. Razeih bends out of frame; comes back up with a bowl holding her "skinny" goldfish.

CLOSE-UP
"Skinny" goldfish in a bowl (in Razieh's hands). The bowl is tipped, "freeing" the fish.

CLOSE-UP
"Tub" of water as the "skinny" fish falls in.

GREAT CHOICES

We hear no dialogue as Ali "convinces" Mother.

We don't *see* Ali go back into the house, instead...

... Razieh stands. This visually "describes" *closer attention* and *anticipation*, and gets us to...

... the **Medium-Shot** of Ali inside. And! Mother glances out at Razieh just before relenting.

Razieh responds to Mother's "yes" by pouring the "skinny" fish into the backyard tub.

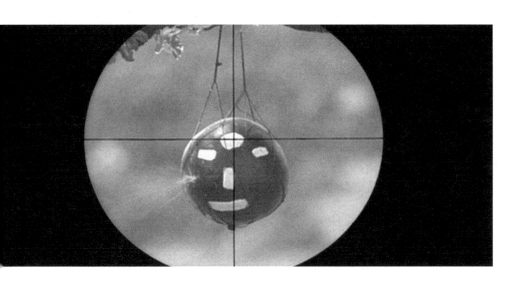

EXPLOITS

Atlantic City: 1981 | 104 minutes | Canada | Louis Malle

STORY

Sally, an oyster bar waitress and aspiring croupier in Atlantic City, New Jersey, is surprised by the arrival of her husband Dave, accompanied by *her* pregnant sister. Dave has brought a bag of cocaine that he filched from a "drug-drop" in a Philadelphia phone booth.

CHARACTERS

Dave

Fred

Patron

SCENE

@ 0:20:09

Interior. Clifton's Bar Bathroom. Day.

"I Don't Do Business with You"

FRED
(to Patron)
Hey man, I need a little space around here...
C'mon, I got business.

(to Dave)
Let's take a look.

DAVE
There you go.

FRED
(inhales some of the powder into his nostril)

Very nice... Whoa! Very nice indeed.
There's been a slight dry spell around here.

DAVE
Dry spell's over... white Christmas... perfect timing.

FRED
Friend called this A.M. Could I help him...
I had to say no. Where'd you get this?

DAVE
I found it in a telephone booth.

FRED
In Philadelphia?

DAVE
How'd you know? Look, I'll help your friend.

FRED
Not looking like that you won't. This is a family town.
Better get yourself cleaned up... a nice leisure suit...
powder blue. Don't need a tie.

DAVE
Maybe you can advance me. You know...
Two hundred dollars, three hundred!
You know I'm good for it.

FRED
This is a very tight town. I only do business with the
people I do business with... the people I do
business with find out I do business with the people
I don't do business with... I can't do business with you.

DAVE
But Boomer in Vegas said...

FRED
I don't do business with Boomer in Vegas.
You look like a fire sale.

DAVE
Look! I've been on the road six weeks okay?
Clean me up, and I'm a fucking Prince Charles.
You won't help me? Look! I'm cutting you in!

FRED
(writing on a slip of paper)
I sure would like to help my friend. But remember!
I don't do business with you!

(Fred flushes the slip into the toilet)

DAVE
(Dave reaches into the bowl,
grabbing the slip before it goes down)
SHIT!

SCENE VALUE

This scene furnishes the impetus for the story/plot/themes, bringing all the characters together. Because of Fred's "warnings" and "rejection," Dave seeks the help of a has-been gangster, Lou Pascal. Dave uses Lou's apartment to "cut" and store the cocaine, and "hires" Lou to make deliveries. This is central to the plot formation. Lou takes possession of the stolen dope when Fred "tips off" drug dealers who show up in Atlantic City, kill Dave, and then pursue Lou and Sally to recover the cocaine.

TEXT
While Fred is "the man to see" in Atlantic City, the word is out about the stolen cocaine. The quality of the cocaine is top notch. But Dave is not!

SUBTEXT
Dave is desperate for cash. He is careless and naïve — it may not be safe for him in Atlantic City.

He is such a pathetic amateur that he doesn't recognize that he is in serious jeopardy. He misjudges whose side Fred is on; supposing that "cutting" Fred in will shield him.

SET-UPS

LONG-SHOT
Dave and Fred enter the bathroom. Fred escorts Patron out. The camera follows the action, moving in to a **Close-Up** as Dave opens the bag of dope, and Fred takes a sniff, crosses the room, and checks his eyes in the mirror.

MEDIUM-SHOT
Fred entering the toilet stall.

MEDIUM-SHOT
Dave facing Fred at the toilet. He walks to screen left exiting the frame.

MEDIUM-SHOT
From behind Fred. Dave approaches. Fred writes info about a cocaine customer. Camera follows the action to the toilet bowl.

CLOSE-UP

Dave facing Fred at the mirror. The camera moves back to a **Medium-Shot** as Fred enters frame right.

CLOSE-UP

Fred enters the toilet stall.

CLOSE-UP

Dave wraps dope and turns left to face Fred in the toilet stall.

GREAT CHOICES

The choice of a public bathroom for Fred's and Dave's "business" discussion adds to the depiction of "misfit" Dave, and lays bare his desperation as he "chases" Fred around the "grubby office." The *physical life* — handling the dope; taking a pinky sniff; using the toilet; writing and flushing the slip of paper — motivates the *physical action* and is the inspiration for the beautifully simple camera moves: These combine to move the characters (and *audience*) around the entire space of the bathroom.

Note how often the *dialogue*, *physical life*, and *physical action* and camera moves occur simultaneously to great effect.

STORY

Algerian resistance and uprising against French rule.

SCENE

@ 0:11:57

Exterior. Casbah Streets. Day

"You Can't Go Wrong"

CHARACTERS

Ali La Pointe

Boy

Girl with a Basket

French Policeman

Café Owner

Crowd

DIALOGUE

(a boy approaches Ali)
ALI
Beat it!

BOY
Men have two faces.
(the boy hands Ali a letter and turns to leave)

ALI
Wait! Know how to read?

BOY
Yes.

ALI
Here!

BOY
(reading from the letter)

There's a Moorish café, rue Randon, the Casbah.
Magherbi, the owner is an informer. Every evening at
exactly five o'clock a policeman comes by.
He goes in for coffee, exchanges a few words and gets
information. Then he leaves. You are to kill this policeman.

ALI
Not the owner?

BOY
It says the policeman.

ALI
Alright.

BOY
You can't go wrong. Near the café will be a young girl with
a basket. You are to follow the policeman together. At the right
moment she'll give you a gun. All you have to do is shoot.

(Ali takes the gun and moves in front of the policeman)

(the Girl with the Basket tries to stop him)

ALI
(to Girl)
Let go!

(to French Policeman)
So you're scared.

(to street crowd)
Brothers! See what the Organization is doing to this coward.

SCENE VALUE

"You Can't Go Wrong" introduces the Boy to Ali; a relationship that continues to the end.

TEXT

However dedicated Ali is to the cause of the resistance he has much to learn about orders and discipline.

SUBTEXT

It happens that Ali is being "tested" by the Algerian Resistance leadership. They want to be certain that he is not an agent of the French.

The scene embodies a common passion: Adults, children, men and women will struggle to liberate the country from the French colonialists.

SET-UPS

EXTREME LONG-SHOT
Ali chases after the Girl with the Basket.

LONG-SHOT
The camera tilts down from rainy rooftops. A group of men, protected with a shared tarpaulin, moves left across the frame. The camera follows them. A boy "appears" and moves into a **Close-Up**.

LONG-SHOT
The boy's POV of Ali. Boy walks to Ali.

LONG-SHOT
Ali and the Girl with the Basket follow the French Policeman. The camera zooms-in to a **Medium-Shot**. As the two of them "catch up" to the Policeman, the camera zooms-out to a **Long-Shot**. Ali, with pistol in hand, runs to the front of the French Policeman.

LONG-SHOT
Ali, with pistol in hand, runs from behind the French Policeman. Ali stops the French Policeman, pointing the pistol. The camera zooms-in to a **Medium-Shot**. Ali pulls the trigger. The gun does not fire.

LONG-SHOT
The Girl with the Basket runs "into" the fight between Ali and the French Policeman. She picks up the gun and hurries off.

The camera zooms-in to Ali. He hurries after her.

LONG-SHOT

Ali's POV. The Girl with the Basket escapes through an alley-like street.

MEDIUM LONG-SHOT

Ali fights with the French Policeman, knocking him to the street.

MEDIUM-SHOT

Ali and the Boy approach steps; they sit. The camera zooms-in to a **Close-Up** of the Boy.

MEDIUM-SHOT

The French Policeman enters a café. The camera pans right as the French Policeman "joins" the café's owner.

MEDIUM-SHOT

The French Policeman exits the café. The camera follows him, panning right.

MEDIUM-SHOT

Ali's POV. The back of the French Policeman as he walks through the crowded streets.

MEDIUM-SHOT

Ali and the French Policeman fight. The French Policeman falls.

CLOSE-UP

Ali. The Boy approaches him. Ali turns to the Boy. The Boy gives Ali a letter. The Boy begins to walk away; Ali "calls" him back, and returns the letter. They walk to steps — in background — and sit.

CLOSE-UP

Ali watches the French Policeman. He looks back to the Girl with the Basket, then looks forward as he and the Girl walk toward the camera exiting frame right.

CLOSE-UP

A basket on the arm of the Girl with the Basket. A pistol comes out and is given to Ali.

EXTREME CLOSE-UP

Ali turns to boy.

EXTREME CLOSE-UP

Boy.

EXTREME CLOSE-UP

Pistol comes up into frame. Trigger is pulled several times....

The reading of the letter is *integrated* with the confrontation. The instructions simultaneously bring the audience to the French Policeman.

Tension is built via Ali's POV shots as he follows behind the Policeman.

Ali doesn't follow his instructions! An intense surprise — for the audience — that joins yet another surprise for the audience and *Ali*: The gun is not loaded.

This last surprise adds a new twist: Ali and the Girl with the Basket must *fight* to escape.

STORY

Jake Gittes, a Los Angeles private eye, finds himself caught up in a convoluted conspiracy.

SCENE

@ 0:41:51

Exterior. Los Angeles Reservoir. Night.

"Wet & Nosey"

CHARACTERS

Jake Gittes

"Midget" (Man in the White Suit)

Claude

JAKE
Son of a bitch. A damn Florsheim shoe.

"MIDGET"
Hold it there Kitty Cat! Hold it!

JAKE
Hello Claude. Where'd you get the midget.

"MIDGET"
You're a very nosey fella' Kitty Cat huh? You know what happens to nosey fella's? Heh? No? Wanna' guess? Heh? No? Okay…

("Midget" slices open Jake's left nostril)
Next time you'll lose the whole thing? I'll cut it off and feed it to my goldfish! Understand?

JAKE
I understand!

Jake's been hired to investigate a case of marital infidelity. Several peculiar events have occurred. "Wet & Nosey" makes clear that there are serious intrigues underway; and they go well beyond the usual labors of a private eye looking into a case of adultery!

TEXT
The actions (and words) make it clear that Jake — himself — is in formidable peril.

SUBTEXT
The previous (and most immediate) moments point to a scheme involving the distribution of precious water. The location of the scene indicates that the private eye has been watched and "tailed." The knife assault points to severe and powerful people. The line "feed it to my goldfish" maintains notions of water.

The location itself has created an "obstacle course" for Jake: He climbs a fence, climbs back, and is just about to climb over again. This action "mirrors" the undercover dilemma Jake faces.

LONG-SHOT

A man in a white suit approaches. A second man enters frame right and they move into a **Close-Up.** The second man exits screen left. The man in white pulls a switchblade knife and points it forward. He brings the blade back. He looks down.

MEDIUM-SHOT

Jake walks along a chain-link fence. The camera moves with him to frame right. Jake stops and begins to climb the fence. He turns in response to a voice. The "man in white" enters into frame right. We see Jake from over the man in white's left shoulder. Claude comes into frame, punches Jake in the gut, and holds him. The switchblade knife moves to Jake's face stopping in his left nostril. It cuts him, and Claude drops him to the ground.

CLOSE-UP

Feet walk toward camera as it moves (back) with them. One foot wears a wet shoe, the other a wet sock.

CLOSE-UP

Jake on the ground with bleeding nose. Claude's legs are in the background. He kicks Jake.

The location keeps the topic of water "on the (audience's) brain."

The Man in White's entrance enhances tension: He moves from the background into the foreground. This move "expands" the illusion of real-space in the two-dimensional presentation of film.

Jake's getting drenched seconds before, and the loss of his expensive shoe nicely connect "wet" and foreshadow "nosey." That is, Jake has been symbolically crippled by the "running wild" water, left hobbling on "one good foot."

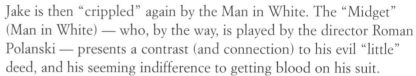

Jake is then "crippled" again by the Man in White. The "Midget" (Man in White) — who, by the way, is played by the director Roman Polanski — presents a contrast (and connection) to his evil "little" deed, and his seeming indifference to getting blood on his suit.

The last shot: Jake on the ground — and bloody — makes for a perfect scene exit for the next scene's *entrance*.

STORY

Right-wing French Army officers hire an assassin — code named Jackal — to kill French President Charles de Gaulle after several of their own attempts fail. The "plot" is discovered; and international intelligence services and government agencies cooperate in an attempt to find the assassin before he can kill the President.

SCENE

@ 0:58:27

Exterior. Italian Country Side. Day.

"Melon"

CHARACTER

The Jackal

SCENE VALUE

This is a weapons test following the Jackal's earlier clandestine meeting(s) with an elderly craftsman to "place an order" for a customized, highly portable rifle — and exploding bullets.

SUBTEXT

Every move within the setting (*physical action*) — and object engagement (*physical life*) — communicates the Jackal's expertise, ingeniousness, and calculatingly murderous commitment.

SET-UPS

EXTREME LONG-SHOT

Across a field to a single small tree with, and without, a hanging melon target.

LONG-SHOT

The Jackal's sports car drives from a country road off the "beaten path," and stops. He exits the car, opens the trunk and removes a can of paint, a brush and *rete* (a sausage/cheese stockinette). He takes a whole green melon from the car, inserts it into the *rete*, paints white circles on the melon, and carries it to the trunk. The Jackal takes the custom-built rifle from the trunk: The camera follows with a pan left as the Jackal walks away and toward the single small tree.

LONG-SHOT

The Jackal walking toward the camera from the "distant tree" into a **Medium-Shot** of his legs and rifle with a pan right bringing the Jackal to another tree and a **Long-Shot**, where he sets up his rifle — the camera moves in slightly — takes aim, and fires.

LONG-SHOT

From behind the small tree shows the Jackal approaching. A slight tilt up and zoom-in shows the Jackal "slam" a spike into an overhanging branch, and hang the "target" melon. A slight tilt down and zoom-out continues the shot as the Jackal walks back across the field.

LONG-SHOT

(Slow Motion/High Speed) from behind the hanging melon. The melon is "hit" and explodes.

MEDIUM-SHOT

The Jackal firing a shot, adjusting the scope with a screwdriver, firing again.

CLOSE-UP

Reverse-side screwdriver adjustment to the scope.

CLOSE-UP

"Special (exploding) bullet" being unwrapped; the camera follows it into the chamber, and tilts up to the Jackal's eye at the scope; and the rifle is fired.

CLOSE-UP

The Jackal's face walking toward the camera, and he exits screen left.

CLOSE-UP

A green melon being painted with white ovals; when complete, the Jackal carries it and exits screen right.

POV (POINT OF VIEW) SHOT through scope shows the melon with a painted "face," and bullet "misses" and the "perfect head hit."

GREAT CHOICES

The previous scene ended with the Jackal driving away from a busy downtown area with the just-purchased melon "sitting" in the passenger seat of his sport's car.

"Melon" opens on the **Extreme Long-Shot** across the field, with the small tree centered. The next cut takes us to a **Close-Up** of the melon being painted. The Jackal is *already* at the "chosen site" for his test.

A cut from the melon painting **Close-Up** takes us immediately to a **Long-Shot** of the Jackal getting his rifle from the trunk of his sport's car.

The Close-Up of the Jackal's face walking toward the camera allows for a feel of "real time" while compressing the actual time to cross the field.

Compressing time is also accomplished on the walk back to the "set-up the rifle tree" by beginning with the pan right in **Medium-Shot** of legs and rifle.

The Jackal's walk back in *measured strides* is a touch that enhances the **subtext**.

The POV (Point Of View) Shots of the melon *through the scope* are used with *one* additional cut back to the **Extreme Long-Shot** of the "melon tree" to *re-emphasize* distance.

The Jackal's use of the melon; cigarette; rope brace for the rifle; screwdriver, and unwrapping the bullet, "display" the Jackal's "calculating professionalism": His handling of objects — *physical life* — shape the audience's emotional engagement.

Note the Jackal's severe gaze at the target — after his first "miss" — while making a scope adjustment. This moment, along with the fact that we never *see* the rifle being fired, captivate and grip the audience.

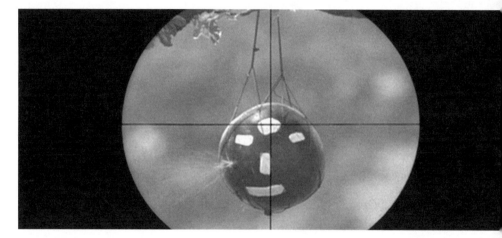

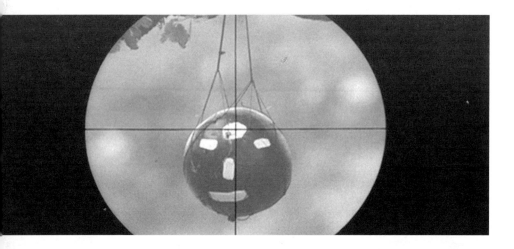

Four cuts of the melon — as seen through the scope — are used. On the third there is *no* rifle shot:

This cut "allows" for the reverse-side screwdriver adjustment cut without a 180-degree break; and dramatically sets up the "bull's-eye" hit.

And then! The "special bullet" is loaded and… the melon explodes!

The choice of a melon as a target is doubly brilliant: The audience might suspect its purchase has something to do with its refreshing summer flavor; and the Jackal can drive off with a perfectly innocent target!

There is but a simple bird ambiance sound track to go along with the "sync" sounds initiated by the Jackal: painting the melon; footsteps; hanging the target; setting the rope brace for the rifle; rifle shots and melon hits; loading the exploding bullet; and the final melon "hit."

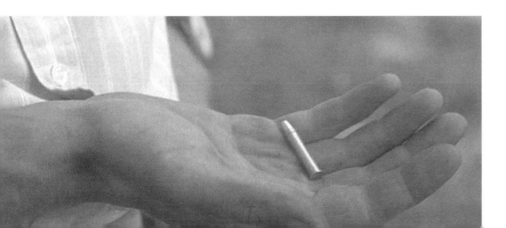

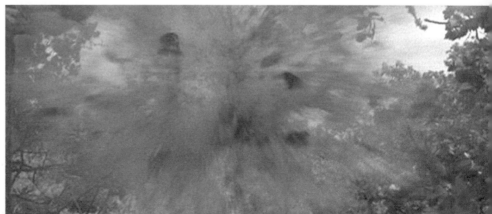

STORY

On a sweltering August day Sonny and Sal get trapped inside a Brooklyn, N.Y. bank during their amateurish attempt at robbery.

SCENE

@ 0:51:02

Interior/Exterior. Bank. Day.

"Who Fired That Shot?"

CHARACTERS

Sonny

Sal

Bank Manager

Bank Tellers

Detective Sgt. Moretti

Police

Street Crowd

SONNY
What's wrong with her?

TELLER #1
There's no air in here.

TELLER #2
What happened to the air-conditioning?

TELLER #1
I'm sorry…

SONNY
Where's the air-conditioning?

MANAGER
The basement.

(Sonny walks to screen left; to an office where Sal is seated)

SONNY
Sal! I'm gonna' check the air-conditioning…
I'll be right back!

SAL
Sonny!

(Sal hurries after Sonny)

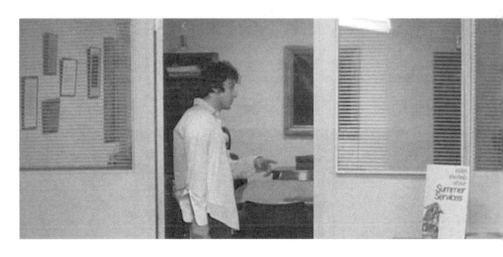

SONNY
What?

SAL
I never been up in an airplane before....

SONNY
So? I mean it's safe... it's like a car...
It's safer than a car. It's all right Sal.

(Sonny turns and walks to screen right)

SONNY
I'm gonna go check it now.

(Sonny and the Bank Manager go to the back)

(Sonny hears a squeaky noise coming from outside the bank's back door)

SONNY
Sal!

SAL
What?

SONNY
They're coming in the back!

SAL
(to the tellers)

In the vault… come on! Move!

(Sonny hurries to the back door, rifle at the ready)

SONNY
(to Bank Manager)
Back… get back!

BANK MANAGER
No, no. Don't… don't… don't!

(gunshot)

(interior & exterior screaming and scrambling)

DETECTIVE SGT. MORETTI
Who fired that shot? Who fired the shot?

Sonny? Sonny! Get me that bullhorn. Sonny? Bullhorn!

(through the bullhorn)

Hey Sonny! Come on out Sonny! Sonny!

CROWD
(in a mocking "sing-song" tone)
Son… ny!

DETECTIVE SGT. MORETTI
Shit! That's all I need… Sonny!!!

CROWD
Son… ny!!!

SCENE VALUE

Sonny believes that he and Detective Sgt. Moretti are on the verge of an agreement: He'll turn over the hostages — one at a time — and the police will provide transportation to JFK International Airport, and a jet flight out of the country.

The chaos of this scene — and the subsequent uncertainty of Sonny (and the F.B.I.) about the "trust" placed in Moretti — gives incentive to the F.B.I. to "take over" the negotiations from the Brooklyn Detective.

TEXT
The early moments of the scene reinforce our affection for Sonny: He is considerate of the teller's discomfort, and gently reassuring about Sal's anxiety.

SUBTEXT
The actions (and text) sustain the volatility of the "hostage stand-off" situation.

SET-UPS

EXTREME LONG-SHOT
Above-angle on crowd. They respond to the "shot" and run for cover.

EXTREME LONG-SHOT
Back of bank as officer is lowered toward the bank's back door. A "shot" cues the cops to duck for cover. The officer being lowered is hoisted back up.

EXTREME LONG-SHOT
Cops on the street "hear the shot." They dive for cover, then get their guns at the ready.

EXTREME LONG-SHOT
Detective Sgt. Moretti comes out of the barber shop. He stops behind a parked car. He gets a bullhorn.

LONG-SHOT
A teller sits in a chair. She is feeling faint. Another teller stands behind her, and still another fans her with a sheet of paper. Sonny enters screen left. He makes his way to a small office to "check in" with Sal about the loss of air-conditioning. The camera moves in to a **Close-Up** as Sal moves toward Sonny. Sonny makes his way to the back of the bank with the manager, moving into the background as the camera pans right into a **Long-Shot**.

LONG-SHOT
Back door area of the bank. The camera follows Sonny panning right as he moves into a **Medium-Shot**. Hearing the squeaky-squeals of a pulley and hoist, Sonny hurries to warn Sal as the camera pans left to follow. Sonny returns, aims his rifle high, and fires! He runs back to the front of the bank.

LONG-SHOT

Sonny comes from the "back door area" as the camera pans left to Sal, then back right as Sal leads the tellers to the vault. Sonny runs past the camera with his rifle, going to the "back door area," then, once again runs past the camera as it follows him right. He leaps over the "fainted teller" and hurries to the bank counter.

LONG-SHOT

Cops standing around their police cars "hear the shot" and take cover.

LONG-SHOT

Pedestrians on the street run for cover.

LONG-SHOT

People on the street flee. Detectives move into a **Medium-Shot** as they crouch for cover.

LONG-SHOT

Low-Angle as the officer is hoisted up and onto the roof.

LONG-SHOT

Sonny hurries behind the counter into a **Close-Up**. The camera follows his movement as he looks to the outside.

MEDIUM-SHOT

One of the tellers faints.

MEDIUM-SHOT

Officer is pulled back up, and onto the roof.

MEDIUM-SHOT

Sal takes cover behind a desk.

MEDIUM-SHOT

Cops "hear" the shot. They rush behind police cars, and draw their weapons.

MEDIUM-SHOT

Journalists and pedestrians take cover.

MEDIUM-SHOT

Cops respond to "shot" and crouch with guns drawn.

MEDIUM-SHOT

Detective Sgt. Moretti comes from the barber shop to a car along the curb. He gets a bullhorn.

MEDIUM-SHOT

A cop leaps from a trash dumpster.

MEDIUM-SHOT

A cop dives for cover falling onto a pile of cartons.

MEDIUM-SHOT

A teller faints. Sonny leaps over her. The teller is helped to the bank vault.

CLOSE-UP

Window above the bank's back door. It gets shot out.

CLOSE-UP

Two tellers are watching TV. They hurry from their seats moving to screen right.

GREAT CHOICES

A great construction in contrasts: The slow-moving somberness — capturing the oppressive heat inside the bank — explodes into bedlam!

There is no "forgetting" all that transpires in the fateful instant of the gunshot: The intercutting returns the audience — again and again — to an array of actions both exterior and interior: The Policeman scurrying up the bank building's side to journalists, bystanders, hostages, and robbers ducking for cover. This broadens the force of the scene.

There is a marvelous creation of "real-time" action as Sonny runs from "location" to "location," background to foreground.

STORY

An imaginative tale of a twelve-year-old boy growing up in a chillingly dysfunctional family in the slums of Montreal.

SCENE

@ 01:16:23

Interior. Bathroom/Air Shaft. Day.

"Bubble Bath Revenge"

CHARACTERS

Grandfather

Léolo

SCENE VALUE

This is a scene of fanciful justice! Earlier in the film, we witnessed — along with Léolo — Grandfather's bathroom "meeting" with pubescent neighbor Bianca for sensual favors. Léolo was repulsed, incensed, and sexually stirred. Add this to other humiliations committed by Grandfather, and Léolo is left no option.

SUBTEXT

"Bubble Bath Revenge" is so absurdly improbable that it raises the likelihood of fantasy. Léolo *imagines* destroying Grandfather — with cruel and unusual punishments — as part of his desire to *break out* from his neighborhood, and demented family.

SET-UPS

EXTREME LONG-SHOT

Grandfather in the bathtub. The noose drops. He struggles. He is "hoisted" upward.

LONG-SHOT

Grandfather in bathtub. Camera moves in to a **Medium-Shot**. Noose drops over his neck, and all of the physical actions are portrayed.

LONG-SHOT

Upside Down. Grandfather's POV. Léolo opens the trap door dropping the noose. Zoom-in and hold on a **Medium-Shot** and then a **Close-Up**.

LONG-SHOT

Grandfather from the foot of the bathtub. The noose drops around his neck, and he fights to free himself.

LONG-SHOT

Low-Angle. Looking up at Léolo "getting to work." He moves toward the camera to free the weight.

LONG-SHOT

Léolo cautiously walks in the air shaft to free the jammed weighted canvas bag.

LONG-SHOT

Pulley.

LONG-SHOT

Air shaft.

MEDIUM-SHOT

Léolo in air shaft. Looks up to the pulley. Looks all the way down the air shaft, then struggles to free the weighted canvas bag.

MEDIUM-SHOT

Léolo at the bottom of the air shaft, knocked unconscious.

MEDIUM-SHOT

Pulley.

MEDIUM-SHOT

Air shaft.

MEDIUM-SHOT

Léolo's trying to kick the canvas bag down into the air shaft. Camera moves right along the 2x4 board, then back left. The bag slides, but is jammed at the air shaft wall.

MEDIUM-SHOT

Weighted canvas bag sliding along 2x4.

MEDIUM-SHOT

Low-Angle. Looking up at "struggling" Léolo.

MEDIUM-SHOT

Low-Angle on Léolo. He leaps for the rope.

CLOSE-UP

Trap door over the bathroom is opened. Rack focus shot from above into a **Long-Shot** of Grandfather. Noose is dropped, and Grandfather is "hoisted" upward. Zoom-in and hold on Léolo's POV.

MEDIUM-SHOT

Grandfather upside down. Léolo's POV.

EXTREME CLOSE-UP

Grandfather in tub. Noose drops around his neck. He tries to get it off.

EXTREME CLOSE-UP

Léolo. Looking down the airshaft carefully making his way to screen right. He jumps for the rope.

EXTREME CLOSE-UP

2x4 brace comes free, leaving bent nails.

EXTREME CLOSE-UP

Hook holding the pulley, which holds the rope, which holds the weighted canvas bag.

A brilliant portrayal of a child's dream of revenge: The intricately creative scheme includes all its messy clumsiness.

With all of Léolo's wonderful calculations — he is even able to "hit his mark" with the noose on his first try — lots of glitches occur nevertheless.

These *unforeseen obstacles* add to the macabre humor, suspense, and daring. Take note of the "visual logic" in the structure of the (many) shots…

… and how the danger to Léolo is constantly reinforced via reminders of the height of the airshaft.

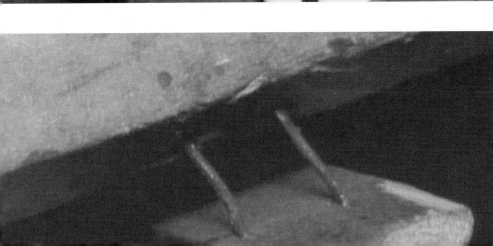

Seven Beauties: 1976 | 115 minutes | Italy | Lina Wertmüller

STORY

The gruesomely uncanny escapades of Pasqualino Frafrusco,
a small-time crook in World War II Naples.

CHARACTERS

Pasqualino

Dead Potono

SCENE

@ 0:48:21

Interior/Exterior. Potono's Bedroom. Day.

"Chopping Eighteen Carat Potono"

PASQUALINO

*(talking to himself as he prepares to chop
Potono's body for disposal)*

Oh God. He's so ugly. Wait a minute here.

(Potono discharges numerous farts when moved)

Even dead you are a pig. Just a big bag of wind.
I knew it. Damn it.

SCENE VALUE

Pasqualino has returned to get rid of Potono's body after shooting
him earlier to avenge his sister's lost honor — she was a working
prostitute for Potono.

SET-UPS

EXTREME LONG-SHOT
Wrapped body lies across the table. Pasqualino sits on the bed,
drinking from a bottle of Cinzano. He puts the bottle down and
stares at Potono's body.

LONG-SHOT
Pasqualino's POV: Potono's sheet wrapped body lies across
a table.

LONG-SHOT
High-Angle: Pasqualino wraps and lifts the body to get it onto
the "operating table."

LONG-SHOT
Extreme Low-Angle looking up. Pasqualino struggles with the
body. He falls into a **Close-Up**.

LONG-SHOT
Ground level. Camera follows action.

MEDIUM-SHOT
Pasqualino tries to lift the body.

MEDIUM-SHOT
Pasqualino can't go through with the dismembering. The camera
zooms-out to a **Long-Shot** as he bumps his head on the bed board,
and despondently sits on the bed. He takes another drink…

MEDIUM-SHOT
The camera follows Pasqualino from the table back to the suitcase
of instruments.

MEDIUM-SHOT

Exterior along wall. A suitcase comes out of a window. It is bulky and tied, being lowered by a rope with a hook at its end. The camera follows it down along the wall. It reaches two other bulky tied suitcases already on the ground. The camera follows the hook back up and into the window. Pasqualino tries exiting "ass first." He re-enters the window, and exits forward. (Note the *jump cut* to get him exiting sooner.)

CLOSE-UP

Above ceiling light fixture. The camera zooms out as an axe lifts into frame. The zoom continues to a **Long-Shot** as Pasqualino is unable to chop!

CLOSE-UP

Pasqualino's face on table, as he works to pull the body.

CLOSE-UP

Axes and other "chopping devices" in a suitcase. The camera zoom-out to Pasqualino as he takes a bottle of Cinzano from the suitcase, and drinks a good gulp. The camera follows him into a **Medium-Shot** at the head of a bed as Pasqualino lifts and wraps the dead Potono. The camera moves out to follow the action.

CLOSE-UP

The face of Potono as Pasqualino wraps the bed sheet over the head.

CLOSE-UP

Pasqualino sits on the bed. He is crestfallen; he looks across the room.

CLOSE-UP

Pasqualino's face. He lifts the axe…

CLOSE-UP

The feet of the body are placed in a basin of sawdust. The camera follows to a **Medium-Shot** as Pasqualino moves to the suitcase.

GREAT CHOICES

There is a silent comedy slapstick-like approach, with great *physical actions* and mishaps. This creates a mesmerizing — yet repugnant — humor.

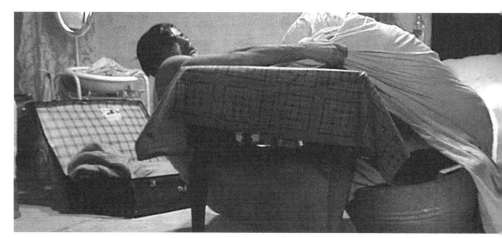

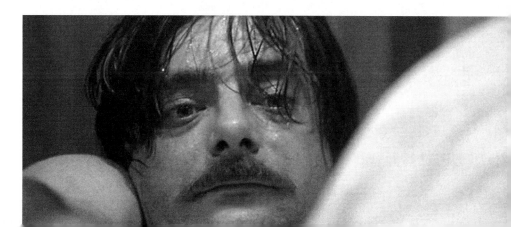

The details are engaging:

A bottle of Cinzano for nerve!

A basin of sawdust to absorb blood!

In the end we see *no chopping; no blood*.... but rather...

... the job is finished; and fit-to-bust suitcases are lowered by rope, out a window, onto the street.

STORY

Three men join together to prospect for gold in the rugged, bandit-controlled mountains of Mexico.

SCENE

@ 0:25:58

Exterior. Sierra Madre Mountains. Day.

""Fool's Gold"

CHARACTERS

Dobbs

Curtain

Howard

DOBBS
Hey! If there was gold in them mountains,
how long would it have been there?
Millions and millions of years wouldn't it?
What's our hurry?
A couple of days more or less
ain't gonna make a difference.

(Curtain comes back to sit with Dobbs)

CURTAIN
Remember what you said back in Tampico about
having to pack an old man on our back?

DOBBS
That was when I took him for an ordinary
human being. Not part goat.

Look at him climb will ya?

CURTAIN
What gets me is how he can go all
day long without any water.

DOBBS
Maybe he's part camel too!

CURTAIN
If I'd known what prospecting meant I'd of stayed
in Tampico and waited for another job to turn up.

DOBBS
Hey! Look at this glitter. It's yellow too… like…

CURTAIN & DOBBS
Gold!

CURTAIN
Howard! Howard! Howard! Howard!

Come back, we found something!

DOBBS
(pouring water over the rock)
Hey! Look! Hey look! Here's a vein of it here
in this rock. Look here! It's all around!

CURTAIN
It glitters here!

DOBBS
Gold is shiny! It glitters like that.
We struck it Curtain! Look!
From the look of things we struck it rich.
Look! It's all over here...

CURTAIN
We found a... whataya call it?

DOBBS
A mother lode! Howard. Howard. Come over here!
(Pours water on the rock.)
Look at this rock... it's full of gold. Veins of it!

HOWARD
That wouldn't pay your dinner for a carload.

DOBBS
That ain't gold?

HOWARD
Pyrites. Fool's gold. Oh! Not that there ain't
plenty of the real stuff hereabouts…
walked over it four or five times.
Place yesterday looked like rich diggings, but
the water for washing the sand
was eleven miles away; too far!
The other places… well not enough gold
to pay us a good day's wages.
The next time you fellas strike
it rich holler for me, will ya?
Before you start splashing water around.

Water's precious… sometimes it could be
more precious than gold!

SCENE VALUE

It is just the beginning of the trio's adventure, and the two younger men cannot "keep up" with "old timer" Howard.

TEXT
The younger men are astounded by Howard's energy and focus; they are also "dangerously" naive.

SUBTEXT
This scene reveals the nascent "defenselessness" of Dobbs and Curtain, along with a quick and lucid demonstration of Howard's experience, knowledge, and wisdom: A foreshadowing of Howard's worth to the expedition. Howard's warning about the slipshod wasting of water foretells of dangers to come from bandits and thirst.

SET-UPS

LONG-SHOT
Howard climbing the mountainside.

LONG-SHOT
Curtain hurries from "gold" to call Howard.

MEDIUM LONG-SHOT
Curtain and Dobbs with burros. Curtain exits frame right. Camera follows Dobbs as he stops to rest. Curtain enters right and joins him to rest.

MEDIUM LONG-SHOT
Howard approaches the camera as he makes his way uphill. He turns, hearing and seeing Curtain in the background, and starts down.

MEDIUM-SHOT
Curtain in the foreground, Dobbs in the background looking upward.

MEDIUM-SHOT
Dobbs in profile.

MEDIUM-SHOT
Curtain full face.

MEDIUM-SHOT
Dobbs watches Howard climb. He looks down "spotting something." He moves to a rock, examining it with his fingers. Curtain comes for a look. He leaves frame to call "Howard." Curtain enters frame right, and the camera follows them, moving and panning right as they examine other rocks, then moving

in to a **Close-Up** of another rock. Curtain and Dobbs hurry off into a **Long-Shot** to check yet another rock in the background. Howard arrives on the scene, then leaves to hike back up the mountain.

MEDIUM CLOSE-UP
Dobbs examines a rock. Curtain enters left, and they hurry to check other rocks.

MEDIUM CLOSE-UP
Howard arrives on the scene. Howard turns and exits frame left.

CLOSE-UP
Sparkling rock. Hands examine its surface.

GREAT CHOICES

In locked-down and camera-follow shots we move about the formation of exposed pyrites: This filming approach captures the excitement of the overly eager greenhorns.

The *physical action* of Dobbs and Curtain, moving from background to foreground, and back again, adds to the rich three-dimensional perspective of the wilderness setting.

STORY

Frank Galvin, an alcoholic "ambulance chasing" lawyer, gets a chance at redemption when he is given a medical malpractice case: Galvin is plaintiff's attorney.

SCENE

@ 0:22:51

Interior. Hospital Ward. Day.

"Polaroid"

CHARACTERS

Frank Galvin

Client

Two Nurses

Other Ward Patients

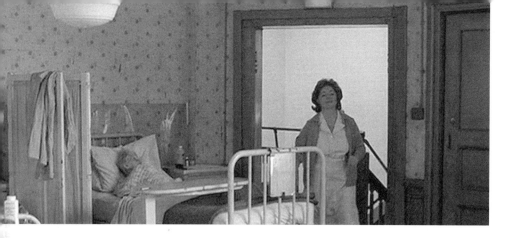

NURSE
Sir! You're not allowed to be in here...
(*she walks into the room toward Galvin*)
...you can't be in here...

GALVIN
I'm her attorney.

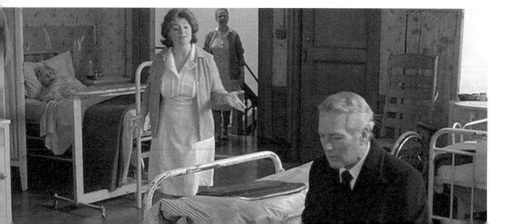

SCENE VALUE

The client is in a permanent vegetative state. Her sister is her legal guardian, and Galvin has been deceiving the sister, concerned only that a settlement will provide him a big payment for little work. In "Polaroid" Galvin comes to recognize that this case — and his efforts as advocate for this client — is likely his last chance at self-respect!

TEXT
The simple few lines go to the heart of the...

SUBTEXT
The extensive pause (beats) *before* Galvin's reply to the nurse imparts in very few words, the conviction that Frank Galvin is "born again" as an advocate for the injured and wronged. Take note: He doesn't respond, "I'm her *lawyer*."

SET-UPS

LONG-SHOT
Galvin enters a hospital ward and takes out a still camera. It's a Polaroid. He takes aim, then moves to the other side of his client's bed, aims and shoots.

He places the ejected picture on the bed as he walks back to the other side.

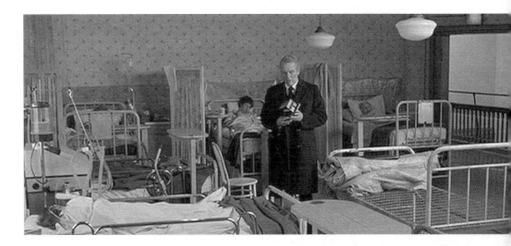

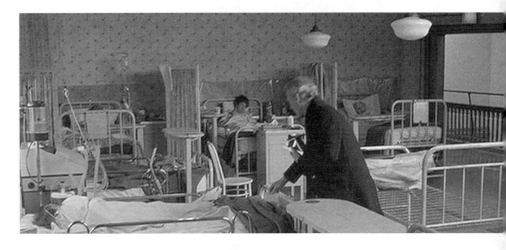

He aims and shoots, then places the second Polaroid picture alongside the first — moving once again to the other side. He pauses looking at his camera. He sits on the side of a bed.

LONG-SHOT
Two nurses appear in the doorway of the ward. One nurse approaches Galvin; the camera moves-out revealing him seated on a bed.

MEDIUM-SHOT
Galvin takes aim, and shoots with his Polaroid camera; places the ejected picture at the foot of his client's bed as he moves to the other side, exiting screen right.

CLOSE-UP

Galvin (on the other side of the bed) takes aim; shoots; (perhaps) exits, and reenters the frame; aims... pauses... looks at his camera, and sits on the side of an empty bed.

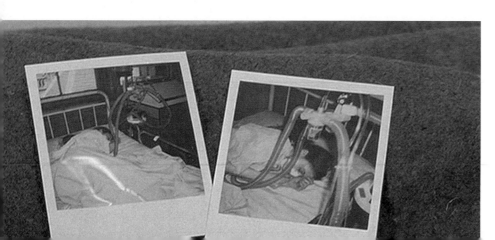

CLOSE-UP (LOW-ANGLE)

Galvin enters the frame; takes aim; but does not take another picture. Instead he pauses and looks at his camera. The camera tilts down to follow as he sits on the side of a bed.

EXTREME CLOSE-UP

Two Polaroid stills slowly "developing" the image of Galvin's client curled in a fetal position with a respirator at her mouth, and tubing crossing her bed.

GREAT CHOICES

The scene *visually* demonstrates Galvin's redemption, as in "I see."

Galvin's use of a *Polaroid* camera — *physical life* — allows the audience to see what Galvin *sees* — as in "We see."

Unexpectedly overcome and overwhelmed, Galvin need not take another picture; he sits on the edge of an empty hospital bed. The several "beats" in silence allow us to "feel" Galvin's transformation.

The sound of the respirator, and the surprisingly similar sound of the Polaroid's shutter and ejected photos, portray the sudden bond between Galvin and his client. Then, a brilliant contrast comes to our ear! The chatting and giggling of two nurses!

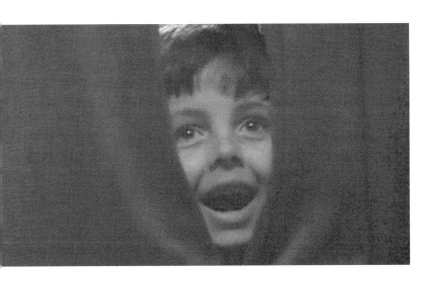

ATTRACTIONS

STORY

At the onset of World War I, Rose and Charlie flee German-occupied East Africa in a ramshackle steam boat.

SCENE

@ 1:40:55

Exterior. *Louisa's* Deck/In the Water. Day.

"Last Request"

CHARACTERS

Charlie

Rose

Captain

First Officer

Louisa Crew

DIALOGUE

CAPTAIN
Noose!

CHARLIE
Wait a minute. Captain…

CAPTAIN
Yes?

CHARLIE
Will you grant us a last request?

CAPTAIN
What is it?

CHARLIE
Marry us.

CAPTAIN
What?

CHARLIE
We want to get married. Ship captains
can do that; can't they?

CAPTAIN
Yes!

ROSE
Why Charlie… what a lovely idea.

CAPTAIN
What kind of craziness is this?

CHARLIE
Oh, come on captain, it'll only take a minute.
It'll mean such a lot to the lady.

CAPTAIN
Very well, if you wish it absolutely.
What are the names again?

CHARLIE
Charles.

ROSE
Rosie… Rose.

CAPTAIN
Do you Charles take this woman to be your
lawful wedded wife?

CHARLIE
Yes sir!

CAPTAIN
Do you Rose take this man to be
your lawful wedded husband?

ROSE
I do.

CAPTAIN
By the authority vested in me by Kaiser Wilhelm II,
I pronounce you man and wife.
Proceed with the execution.

(Explosions shake the Louisa. *All abandon ship*)

CHARLIE
What happened?

ROSE
We did it Charlie… we did it!

CHARLIE
But how?
(sees a piece of the African Queen)
Well…whataya think!? Are you alright Mrs. Allnut?

ROSE
Wonderful. Simply wonderful.
And you Mr. Allnut?

CHARLIE
Pretty good… for an old married man!

ROSE
I'm all turned around Charlie.
Which way is the east shore?

CHARLIE
The way we're swimming old girl!
(singing)
There once was a bold fisherman….

SCENE VALUE

This is the concluding scene(s) of the film.

It makes "official" the love between Rose and Charlie: A love that has burgeoned through their shared difficulties, and scheme to destroy the German warship *Louisa*.

There is irony in that the wrecked *African Queen* not only fulfills Rose and Charlie's scheme to destroy the German warship, but also saves their lives.

TEXT
The German Captain is impatient with Rose and Charlie. He wants the hanging done swiftly.

SUBTEXT
Charlie is somewhat embarrassed to make his "last request" and so he represents it as *good manners*: It is not so much that he wants to be married before he dies, but that he is "willing to go through with it" for "the lady."

EXTREME LONG-SHOT
The capsized *African Queen* "floats" in the foreground, her "homemade torpedo" pointing toward the oncoming *Louisa*.

EXTREME LONG-SHOT
Two figures in the water after the *Louisa* sinks.

LONG-SHOT
Pan down main mast from behind Rose and Charlie. Ceremony performed. Nooses "applied;" chaos begins.

LONG-SHOT
Rose and Charlie float and find a piece of the *African Queen*. They swim toward shore, cheerfully singing.

LONG-SHOT
Along the railing as seamen flee the *Louisa*.

LONG-SHOT
The *Louisa* capsizes, as crewmen scramble along her bottom.

LONG-SHOT
The *Louisa's* propeller exposed.

MEDIUM-SHOT
First Officer.

MEDIUM-SHOT
The camera moves-in, past the Captain to Rose and Charlie.

MEDIUM-SHOT
The camera follows Charlie and Rose through smoke. They "disappear," exiting frame left.

MEDIUM-SHOT
Boiler room crewmen flee.

MEDIUM-SHOT
Low-Angle looking up at *Louisa's* side. Crewmen leap into the water.

MEDIUM-SHOT
Ship's hatch as crewmen rush to the deck.

MEDIUM-SHOT
Rose and Charlie find a piece of the *African Queen*.

MEDIUM-SHOT
Captain and First Mate in the water.

MEDIUM CLOSE-UP
Charlie and Rose.

CLOSE-UP
Captain.

CLOSE-UP
Rose.

CLOSE-UP
Captain and Charlie.

CLOSE-UP
Rosie and Charlie as crewmen apply nooses. Smoke and chaos begin.

GREAT CHOICES

A wonderful simultaneous connection and contrast: Formal ceremonies: wedding and execution…

… both presided over by the captain of the *Louisa*!

The gathering of the crew and officers for the execution (and wedding) provides important plausibility: No one sees the *African Queen* ahead.

The use of dramatic irony — we see the *African Queen* as the *Louisa* approaches — builds the kind of suspense common in movie serials: Will the torpedo hit the *Louisa* before Charlie and Rose are hanged?

Yes! The *Louisa* is sunk. Charlie and Rose are saved!

STORY

An epic tale in 1943 (World War II) Burma; British prisoners (POWs) — under Japanese control — build a railroad bridge across a river's gorge.

SCENE

@ 2:28:31

Exterior. Kwai River. Day.

"Something Odd is Going On"

CHARACTERS

Colonel Nicholson

Major Clipton

Japanese Colonel Saito

Lieutenant Joyce

Major Shears

Major Warden

Scout & Aides

Japanese Soldiers

NICHOLSON

If Saito's information is correct, the train should
be along in about five or ten minutes.

CLIPTON

If you don't mind sir, I'll watch the ceremony
from up on the hill.

NICHOLSON

Why? You'll get a better view from the bridge.

CLIPTON

It's hard to explain sir, but I'd rather
not be a part of it.

NICHOLSON

As you please… Honestly Clipton! Sometimes
I don't understand you at all.

CLIPTON

As you once said sir, I've got a lot to learn about the army.

NICHOLSON

(walks to bridge and greets Col. Saito)
Good morning!

*(Nicholson hears the train off in the distant jungle.
He becomes suspicious when he notices exposed wire
around the bridge's support timbers)*

SHEARS

(watching Col. Nicholson from across the river)
What's he doing?

NICHOLSON

(returns to Col. Saito)
Colonel! There's something odd going on.
I think we better have another look around
before that train comes across.

*(Nicholson and Saito make their way
from the bridge to the river's bank)*

SCENE VALUE

After initially resisting Colonel Saito's order that he and his men build the bridge for the Japanese military, Nicholson consents, so that, as Commanding British Officer, he might sustain the health and morale of his soldiers.

Major Shears, an escaped former POW, has returned to the River Kwai, leading a team of commandos to destroy the bridge, along with the first Japanese supply train to cross.

This *next-to-last* scene brings an astonishing and fatal reunion to the story's central characters.

TEXT
The dialogue motivates Clipton's trek up the hillside, to observe the "celebration" of the completed bridge.

SUBTEXT
"Something Odd is Going On" illustrates the final moments of Nicholson's bizarre break from reality: He has so intensely focused the bridge's purpose to the *respectability* of his command, that its essential function — with his backing — as aid to the enemy has been lost to him. Major Clipton represents narrator, conscience, witness, and in the end, the voice of perspective and sanity.

EXTREME LONG-SHOT
The Jungle (POV) of Nicholson and Saito.

EXTREME LONG-SHOT
The bridge.

EXTREME LONG-SHOT
Binocular view of Major Warden as he watches Nicholson. There is a tilt down as Nicholson leans to "inspect" the bridge's timber supports, and a tilt up as Nicholson walks toward Saito.

LONG-SHOT
Nicholson and Clipton walk toward the camera. The camera moves-back with them into a **Medium-Shot**. They stop. Nicholson exits screen left; Clipton pauses, then exits screen right.

LONG-SHOT
High-Angle shot as Clipton climbs a hill and sits on a tree stump.

LONG-SHOT
Nicholson enters frame left. He clears a piece of "debris" from the tracks.

LONG-SHOT
Nicholson approaches the camera into a **Close-Up**. He reacts to train "whistle."

LONG-SHOT
Nicholson's POV. A broken tree trunk juts out of the river. A wire is exposed, caught on the tree.

MEDIUM-SHOT
Along the bridge railing as Nicholson enters screen right. He leans on the railing. The camera moves-in to a **Medium Close-Up** as Nicholson "spots" something. Nicholson walks away into a **Long-Shot**.

MEDIUM-SHOT
Nicholson's POV of wire entangled along bridge supports.

MEDIUM-SHOT
Nicholson enters frame right, walks onto the bridge, moving into a **Long-Shot**.

MEDIUM CLOSE-UP
Major Warden watching through binoculars.

MEDIUM-SHOT
The camera moves left with Nicholson.

MEDIUM-SHOT
Low-Angle view of Clipton sitting on a tree stump.

CLOSE-UP
Lt. Joyce hiding downstream. He reacts to the train "whistle."
The camera follows his hands as he bends and lifts the plunger
on a detonator.

MEDIUM-SHOT
Major Warden prepares a mortar.

MEDIUM-SHOT
Major Shears watches.

MEDIUM-SHOT
Nicholson enters frame left as he moves to the opposite railing.
He looks up and around. He walks away from the camera and
stops. He looks to screen right....

CLOSE-UP
Colonel Saito.

CLOSE-UP
Nicholson enters frame right. The camera is behind him; he stops,
looks to screen right. He cups his hands above his eyes — shielding
them from the sun — to look out to the river. He turns and walks
away.

GREAT CHOICES

Extraordinary use of mounting tension:

The slow methodical last check of the bridge by the self-satisfied Col. Nicholson.

The commandos watching helplessly as the river's "low tide" has "exposed" their plans.

Nicholson sees something. Nicholson's suspicions are aroused. Nicholson is alarmed!

The audience is both observer and participant, "moved" back
and forth across the river:

Behind the binoculars; on the bridge; downstream with the
plunger/detonator, and listening for the approaching train.

Accompanying Nicholson and Saito to "have another look around."

STORY

Dora, a sixty-seven-year-old retired teacher, promises to bring nine-year-old Josue to his estranged father who lives in a village somewhere in northeastern Brazil. Josue's mother has been killed in an accident; and life for a homeless boy on the streets of Rio is exceedingly dangerous.

SCENE

@ 0:00:01

Interior. Train Station. Day.

"Letter for Josue"

CHARACTERS

Dora

Josue

Mother

Featured Commuters

Station Crowds

WOMAN

My heart belongs to you. No matter what you've done I still
love you. I love you. While you're locked in there all those years,
I'll be locked up out here, waiting for you.

MAN

I want to send a letter to a guy who cheated me. Mr. Zè Amaro.
Thank you for what you did to me. I trusted you, and you
cheated me. You even took the keys to my apartment.

MOTHER

Dear Jesus, you're the worst thing to happen to me. I'm only
writing because your son Josue asked me to. I told him you're
worthless and yet he still wants to meet you.

DORA

Address?

MOTHER

Jesus de Paiva. Bom Jesus do Norte. Pernambuco.

The opening moments of the film and we get right to the story while, at the same time, the "moments" bond the *central* characters and the place.

TEXT
In this large public place, people in need of Dora's services must be willing to "shamelessly" divulge the most personal of situations — and emotions. And! the fact that they are illiterate.

SUBTEXT

There is a glaring correlation to the relationship of a parishioner and a father confessor. With the busyness of the station, and the large number of people who are in need of Dora's help, there is a strong impression that Dora tries to protect herself from any emotional involvement with her "clients": She "just does her job." But! With Josue (and his mother) something has "touched" her; she will remember this moment.

SET-UPS

LONG-SHOT
Looking down length of a train. Passengers begin to exit.

LONG-SHOT
Gate with passengers approaching.

LONG-SHOT
Crowded station.

LONG-SHOT
People entering and exiting tunnel-way of the station.

LONG-SHOT
Dora's POV. Mother and Josue leave. The camera pans left following them.

MEDIUM-SHOT
Mother and Josue.

MEDIUM-SHOT
Dora. At the end of the shot the camera moves right as Dora watches Mother and Josue leaving.

MEDIUM-SHOT
Over Dora's right shoulder as Mother and Josue leave the table.

CLOSE-UP
Woman.

CLOSE-UP
Man.

CLOSE-UP
Mother and Josue.

CLOSE-UP
Josue over Dora's right shoulder.

CLOSE-UP
A box of stamps and pens. Josue's toy top scrapes the box side.

CLOSE-UP
Legal pad with (Dora's) hand taking dictation.

CLOSE-UP
Slightly above-angle on envelope. Dora is filling in an address.

GREAT CHOICES

The opening lines are played in voice over: A beginning that raises our interest and curiosity, and then increases both when we meet the Woman (in the first close-up), and hear her mournful "story." The "time" taken before we learn the specifics of the state of affairs in the train station is alluringly effective.

The scene's tenor is evocative of a *Catholic confessional*: Dora as Confessor, conveying Josue's request to Jesus, the Father.

STORY

An extended flashback to post-World War II rural Italy where Toto and Alfredo begin a friendship of lasting affection, and Father Adelfio acts as censor for the town's movies.

SCENE

@ 0:08:06

Interior. Movie Theatre. Day.

"Ringing Kisses"

CHARACTERS

Salvatore (Toto)

Alfredo

Father Adelfio

FATHER ADELFIO
Alfredo! You can start!

ALFREDO
Here we go again!

(projected image is not framed properly)

FATHER ADELFIO
The frame!

(Alfredo corrects the problem)

SCENE VALUE

This scene is our introduction to Alfredo, the local projectionist, and Father Adelfio's requirement: He will hold the first screening, so as to censor all the movies that arrive in town. The events of this scene embody the legacy of Alfredo and Salvatore's relationship.

TEXT
Father Adelfio is getting a private movie screening.

Much of the "dialogue" in this scene — not included here — is that spoken in the movies being projected and "examined" by Father Adelfio.

SUBTEXT

The church's fear of movie's magic works as an (ongoing) analogy to the expulsion from the Garden following Eve's encounter with the serpent and the apple: The power of knowledge will corrupt the innocent.

Toto, secretly observing from behind the curtain, seems more sophisticated in his openness to the pleasures of the screen, and to the silliness of the Father's ire.

EXTREME LONG-SHOT

Alfredo's POV of Father Adelfio entering the front of theatre. The priest takes his seat. "Lights out," and the projector's beam fills the screen.

EXTREME LONG-SHOT

Looking upward to the projection booth. "Lights out," and a beam of light "fills" the lion's mouth.

LONG-SHOT
High-Angle shot as the priest enters the theatre. The camera follows right. Then tilts upward as Father Adelfio calls to Alfredo in the projection booth.

LONG-SHOT
Alfredo peering through booth window reacting to Father Adelfio's "You can start." "Lights out," projection light beams from the lion's mouth, and Alfredo watches.

LONG-SHOT

Behind Father Adelfio with movie images filling the screen.

LONG-SHOT

Slow move-in to Toto, secretly watching from behind a curtain. The camera "captures" various reactions in **Medium-Shot** and **Close-Up**.

LONG-SHOT

Alfredo in booth watching. Reacting to Father Adelfio, he slips a strip of paper into the turning reel.

LONG-SHOT

Father Adelfio takes his seat. An assistant pulls the shutters closed.

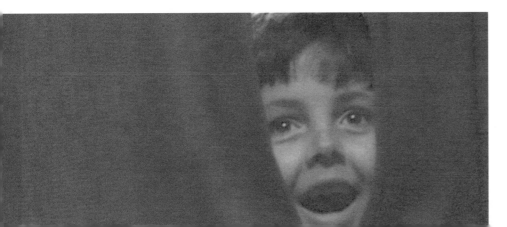

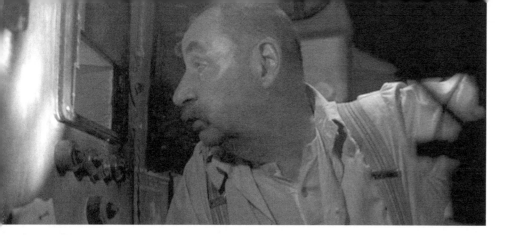

MEDIUM LONG-SHOT

Alfredo in his booth preparing and operating the projector… and continuing actions of the scene.

MEDIUM-SHOT

Alfredo at the projector marking censored moments with paper strips slipped into turning reels.

MEDIUM-SHOT

Alfredo peers through the projection booth window.

MEDIUM-SHOT

From behind the priest: Images on the screen fill the background.

MEDIUM CLOSE-UP

Father Adelfio watching and reacting to movie moments.

CLOSE-UP

Front view of Father Adelfio sitting with a bell at the ready. He reacts to "kissing" moments, and rings the bell signaling a "deletion" for Alfredo.

CLOSE-UP

Alfredo in the projection booth. Camera tilts up to follow as he starts the projector.

CLOSE-UP
Movie images fill frame.

CLOSE-UP
Bell goes into the air and rings!

CLOSE-UP
Bell sits on Father Adelfio's lap; his fingers tap the side.

This scene is a splendid modern example of the vividness of European montage: Via the juxtaposition of images, the characters and their relationships are presented with affection, wit, and intelligence.

STORY

Composer Gustav Aschenbach takes holiday in Venice endeavoring to regain his health. The Italian authorities are concealing an outbreak of cholera.

SCENE

@ 0:22:41

Interior. Hotel Lobby. Evening.

"Beautiful Boy"

CHARACTERS

Gustav

Attractive Family

Beautiful Boy

Governess

Orchestra

Hotel Employees

Hotel Guests

MAÎTRE D' HOTEL
Ladies and Gentlemen! Dinner is served.

SCENE VALUE

Introduction to Gustav's stay in Venice. His encounter with the Beautiful Boy begins a fascination and ultimate fixation underscored in the…

SUBTEXT

The story's theme of beauty and youth launch a mortal anxiety in the old and ill Gustav.

SET-UPS

LONG-SHOT
Orchestra playing in the hotel lobby. The camera pans left and moves in to find Gustav. The camera follows him, panning right. He selects a newspaper and sits in **Medium-Shot**. The camera moves out and pans left.

LONG-SHOT
From behind the Governess and family. They get up. Camera pans right to the approaching mother. The camera follows her left, moving out to a **Medium Long-Shot**; then moving in to a **Close-Up** of the mother.

LONG-SHOT
Looking past Gustav to the dining room. The family passes him. The Beautiful Boy stops, turns, and looks back to Gustav; then the Beautiful Boy exits screen right.

MEDIUM LONG-SHOT
Orchestra plays.

MEDIUM LONG-SHOT
The family gets up to go to the dining room. The camera pans right following them as they pass Gustav.

MEDIUM-SHOT
Pan right and tilt up and down slightly, "finding" the faces of the children.

MEDIUM-SHOT
On Beautiful Boy. The camera pans right to Gustav. The camera moves out, panning left.

MEDIUM-SHOT
Hotel Manager greets people, as the camera follows panning right, and to Gustav in **Long-Shot** as hotel guests move toward the dining room.

CLOSE-UP
Gustav with newspaper, and observing guests in the lobby, especially the Beautiful Boy.

CLOSE-UP
Beautiful Boy. The camera moves out to a **Long-Shot** from behind Gustav. He appears to be getting ready to rise, but he does not.

CLOSE-UP
Beautiful Boy in profile. The camera moves out (and left) to the family in a **Long-Shot**.

GREAT CHOICES

Sitting with the Hotel's complimentary newspaper emphasizes that Gustav is by himself; it also contrasts the lively lobby.

The orchestra music seems to prompt the rhythms and movement of the camera.

When the guests are called to the dining room, Gustav is going to join them — just about to rise from his chair — instead he settles back to "keep an eye" on the Beautiful Boy.

Gustav "secretly" admires the boy.

Gustav remains seated as the Beautiful Boy and his family make their way to the Dining Room.

As the boy approaches the dining room — the last of his family, and the other hotel guests — he stops…

… and slowly turns looking back to Gustav. He knows that Gustav has been "studying" him.

Hiroshima Mon Amour: 1959 | 91 minutes | France | Alain Resnais

STORY

A French actress and a Japanese architect become lovers in the city of nuclear ruin.

SCENE

@ 0:17:57

Exterior/Interior. Hiroshima Hotel. Day.

"Morning After"

CHARACTERS

French Actress

Japanese Architect

Bicyclers

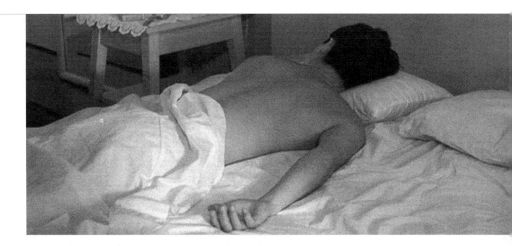

ACTRESS
Coffee?

ARCHITECT
Uh-huh…

ACTRESS
What were you dreaming?

ARCHITECT
I don't know… why?

ACTRESS
Your hands… they move when you're asleep.

ARCHITECT
Sometimes a person dreams without realizing it.

SCENE VALUE

The "Morning After" begins, and sets, the naturalistic presentation of the story, characters, and plot. It follows an extended opening which combines multiple film forms of disturbingly real and surreal images, driven by a relentlessly disturbing melody, and poetic voice over.

The scene is also the introduction to the French Actress' haunting remembrances of Nevers, France.

TEXT

In unassuming dialogue the scene connects East and West: "Coffee?" The French Actress — in a kimono — pours the Architect a cup of coffee from a traditional Japanese teapot.

SUBTEXT

The images connecting the hand of the Architect to the Actress' memory of the dead man present an allegory linking *sleep* and *death*.

LONG-SHOT
High-Angle looking from the roof. Bicyclers ride to screen left.
The camera follows the bicyclers revealing the French Actress.
The camera follows her left to a terrace railing. She climbs over
toward her room, and waits at the terrace doorway.

LONG-SHOT
From inside the hotel room, the Actress approaches the railing and climbs over. She moves into a **Medium-Shot**.

LONG-SHOT
Architect is asleep on his stomach. The fingers on his right hand move.

He awakes; sits up in bed. The camera moves out and to the left as the actress enters frame right.

She pours coffee, kneeling beside the bed.

MEDIUM LONG-SHOT
Architect asleep on his stomach. The fingers of his right hand move.

MEDIUM-SHOT

From the interior of the terrace doorway. Actress moves toward the camera, and rests against the terrace door frame. She smiles and enters the room, moving to frame left.

MEDIUM CLOSE-UP

Over the architect's right shoulder. The actress pours coffee, kneeling beside the bed.

CLOSE-UP

Actress in doorway. She looks downward, then up again with a smile, and enters the room; exiting frame left.

CLOSE-UP

A hand. The camera pans right. We see the bloodied face of a dead soldier. A woman kisses him.

GREAT CHOICES

A powerfully distinct contrast to the opening scene(s): Light/Hope vs. Darkness/Despair.

The Actress *alone* at the outset of "Morning After" initiates a doubt in the mind of the audience: "Was the previous scene a reality, a dream, a nightmare?"

Later we will learn that all three are correct; and additional metaphors tie all three to memories.

Ju Dou: 1990 | 93 minutes | China | Zhang Yimou

Tianging returns to his uncle's cloth dye mill in a Chinese country village after a journey to deliver finished goods. The rich uncle has "purchased" his third wife, Ju Dou. The uncle is abusive to his new wife. Tianging is infatuated by Ju Dou's beauty. Later the uncle leaves the mill to seek help for his sick pack animal. Tianging and Ju Dou are left together.

Ju Dou

Tianging

SCENE

@ 0:28:39

Interior. Dye Mill. Day.

"Letting Loose"

JU DOU
Tianging, are you afraid?

TIANGING
Me afraid?

JU DOU
Then why did you latch your door?
You're a grown man… Am I a wolf?
You think I'll eat you?

TIANGING
My uncle…

JU DOU
He can go to hell.

TIANGING
If someone came by…

JU DOU
That didn't stop you from looking through the hole.

TIANGING
Why didn't you plug it up?

JU DOU
Tianging, I've kept my body for you.

SCENE VALUE

Tianging and Ju Dou make love. This leads to the birth of their baby boy; the Uncle believes that *he* is the father to a son and heir.

TEXT
The dialogue links earlier events: Ju Dou tells Tianging that she knows that he's been watching her bathe. Last night Ju Dou went to Tianging's room, but he locked her out.

SUBTEXT
There is a folk tale atmosphere at work in the scene's complex metaphors: the blood-red pool of "collapsing" cloth; the basket; the driving wooden posts and gears.

The scene adds a "turn" to victim and aggressor; and situates later *dramatic irony*, and rich story *irony* as both mockery, and quirks of fate.

EXTREME LONG-SHOT
Across beam supports, working wooden gears, and posts of the mill, we see Ju Dou, and Tianging seated apart. They are eating.

LONG-SHOT
Ju Dou eating with chop sticks. The camera follows her to Tianging.

LONG-SHOT
Slow-Motion (optically step-printed) tilting up to the drapped colored cloths, and sky.

MEDIUM-SHOT
Tianging eating with chop sticks; Ju Dou enters frame.

CLOSE-UP
Ju Dou's face "falling" into position on mill planking.

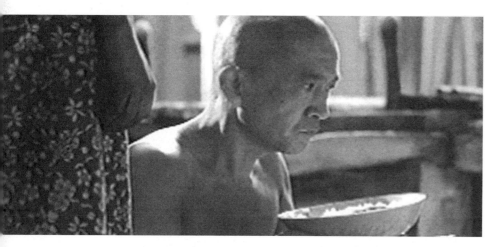

CLOSE-UP

Red-dyed cloth quickly tumbling from the overhead racks back into the vat of dye.

CLOSE-UP

Basket as red cloth is uncontrollably pulled upward.

EXTREME CLOSE-UP

Ju Dou's foot kicking free the wooden "brake" holding a wooden flywheel.

CLOSE-UP

Spinning flywheel.

GREAT CHOICES

An excellent example of *physical action* and *physical life*: The scene opens with Ju Dou and Tianging seated and eating. Sensual *signals* are sent by Ju Dou. She "cleans" her chop sticks with her tongue and lips. Her move toward Tianging is preceded by her adjusting one of her slippers.

Tianging and Ju Dou have dye-stain on their hands: A rich addition to their meal break; and another metaphor for what is about to occur — and a foreshadowing of the couple's approaching misfortunes.

Ju Dou seduces Tianging from behind. He can feel and hear her, but there is no eye-contact until Tianging whirls to take her.

Erotic tempting is enhanced by the repetitive poundings of the working mill.

The sexual act is emphasized with the sounds of the "gone wild" gears, and hammerings of the mill: Ju Dou and Tianging have "let loose" the mill, and their sexual yearnings.

At the conclusion, a wind instrument initiates a haunting reminiscence of a baby's cry, and provides an emotional "intermission" before the next scene.

STORY

The village's "local Fuehrer" appoints his brother-in-law, Tono, to be the Aryan controller of a button shop owned by an elderly Jewish widow. Instead, the decent Tono behaves as Mrs. Lautman's assistant. Finally the entire Jewish population of the village is ordered to prepare for "relocation."

SCENE

@ 1:58:24

Interior. Button Shop. Day.

"It's All Over"

CHARACTERS

Tono

Mrs. Lautman

Woman & Boys

Dog

DIALOGUE

*(Tono forces Mrs. Lautman into a closet
to hide her from his brother-in-law)*
TONO
Mrs. Lautman, you can come out now. It's all over.
*(Tono unlocks the closet door... he opens it...
Mrs. Lautman is dead)*

*(Tono sees a woman taking her son and
his friend into her house)*
WOMAN
Where were you? Come in Danko.

SCENE VALUE

"It's All Over" follows the ordered assembly of the village's
Jews, and precedes the concluding scene, "preparing" the
inspired ending.

TEXT
The camera moves to and through the mystical opening of the
shop's shutters and doors, into the brightness of a gentle and
loving village and world.

SUBTEXT
Tono is overwhelmed by conscience: His unpardonable terror
and panic have contributed to Mrs. Lautman's death.

He is plagued by the camera (the viewer) as "eyewitness."

LONG-SHOT

Tono enters the button shop, and stops at the shop's counter. He turns, responding to an alarm clock's ring. He walks toward the camera and the closet.

LONG-SHOT

Looking out the back door of the button shop. A woman is holding her son, his friend stands behind him. Tono enters into the foreground of frame left, and quickly steps back so as not to be seen. The woman takes both boys inside her house. Tono opens a back door, and calls to his dog; the dog obeys and Tono lets him out, closing and locking the door.

LONG-SHOT

Tono moves under a hook and places the small table there. He drops the rope onto the table and walks toward the front of the shop, passing the camera.

MEDIUM LONG-SHOT

Alarm clock on counter: It rings!

MEDIUM LONG-SHOT

A bureau. The camera pans left. We see Tono sitting at a cabinet. He finds rope. He stands, putting the rope in his pocket. He exits frame right.

MEDIUM LONG-SHOT

Tono's dog comes toward the camera. The camera follows left as the dog exits the back door past Tono. Tono closes and locks the door As he leaves the frame, the camera moves-in toward the door handle.

MEDIUM-SHOT

Tono looks to the closet. The camera follows panning right as Tono goes to the closet, unlocks the door, and taps on it. He moves back toward the counter as the camera follows left, then follows right, and to the closet door. Tono opens the door. He looks inside, steps back closing the door.

MEDIUM-SHOT

A swish pan brings us to Tono. He is sitting in a chair, looking upward. He looks at the camera, and up again. The camera moves left, and tilts up to show a hook jutting from an archway ceiling. Tono enters the frame, pauses, walks to the background, and out of frame; his shadow crosses the ceiling hook.

MEDIUM-SHOT

Tono is sitting and untangling rope. He stands. The camera follows him as he bends to pick up a small table upon which he was sitting. Tono exits frame left. The camera holds on the floor.

MEDIUM-SHOT

Front door looking out. Tono enters frame right. He opens one door, and takes hold and closes the shutters. He locks the door, and as he walks back toward the archway, the camera moves slowly toward the door handle. The camera holds.

CLOSE-UP

The back of Tono as he opens the closet door. The camera tilts down to a **Medium-Shot** of Mrs. Lautman on the floor. She is dead.

CLOSE-UP

Low-Angle from inside the closet. The door opens. Tono looks in and quickly closes the door.

CLOSE-UP

Mrs. Lautman's face. Her eyes open. She is dead.

CLOSE-UP

Closet door handle. The camera moves left around the button shop. It "finds" Tono. He looks at the camera, and "ducks" out of frame, as the camera moves in to the shelves of buttons. The camera begins moving again. It "searches" into Mrs. Lautman's apartment at the back of the shop. It "finds" Tono and moves toward him. He "ducks away," revealing Mrs. Lautman's food preparations for the Sabbath. The camera looks for him yet again, moving left, then right; it finds him, and as he moves away it tilts up to the wall, and centers on two framed photos: Mrs. Lautman and Mr. Lautman. A right swish pan ends the shot.

CLOSE-UP

The small table now tipped. The camera tilts upward to show the closed front doors. The shutters open, letting light into the shop. The front doors open, and the camera moves into the light.

GREAT CHOICES

Tono's death is represented with sensitivity and simplicity.

The "eyewitness" camera is accompanied by chanting: It mercilessly haunts Tono, until desolation and shame make death attractive.

The storytelling strength is derived from the cruelty of Tono's situation: an ambivalent struggle to protect Mrs. Lautman, or to save himself. Neither is accomplished, and yet the directors find a way to end their story with hope.

STORY

Tom falls from the good graces of his guardian and wealthy landowner, Squire Allworthy. Now Tom must make his own way in the world.

SCENE

@ 1:12:08

Interior. Country Inn. Evening.

"Eating"

CHARACTERS

Tom Jones

Mrs. Waters

Inn Patrons & Staff

SCENE VALUE

"Eating" is part of an adventure sequence which includes Tom's encounter with Army Regulars; drinking with them at an inn, and his receiving a head wound in a "disagreement" with a British officer. The next day Tom happens upon the same officer sexually assaulting a woman. Tom rescues her, but Mrs. Waters' clothing is tattered and revealing. As Tom guides her through the countryside his "curiosity" and Mrs. Waters' glances begin to get the better of him. They arrive at the inn.

SET-UPS

LONG-SHOT
In the country inn. A pan to the right reveals Tom and Mrs. Waters seated in a booth.

LONG-SHOT
Tom and Mrs. Waters "hurry" toward the camera and into a **Medium-Shot**; camera pans left as they rush to the privacy of a room, moving into a **Long-Shot** away from the camera.

MEDIUM CLOSE-UP
Tom and Mrs. Waters in profile, they hold their glasses in a toast, and lean closer to each other; finishing a "last glass" of wine. They stare at each other, and hurry from the table.

MEDIUM CLOSE-UP
Tom eating his way "through" a multi-course meal.

MEDIUM CLOSE-UP
Mrs. Waters eating her way "through" a multi-course meal.

GREAT CHOICES

No serving is shown, instead, courses are "served up" by way of cuts — from Tom to Mrs. Waters and back again — which "jump" to each new course.

The meal*time* is greatly compressed: The scene opens with the two *already* served…

... yet the "tasty" seduction stretches into spectacular humor.

Contact — barely physical — occurs only twice during the meal, helping to maintain the "nearness" of the two.

1. Mrs. Waters offers Tom a pinky grip on her wishbone.

2. Tom offers Mrs. Waters an oyster.

The "offerings" cross to and through the frame, and so help the increase in sexual tension.

A simple touch retains the information of the busy surroundings: Tom looks sheepishly to see if any of the inn's customers — or staff — are watching.

The last moments at the table — drinking down the meal — "cues" harpsichord music…

… which releases the bursting Tom and Mrs. Waters in an uncontrollable dash to a bedroom.

ADDED ATTRACTIONS

Assignments for Discussion

Consider the **Location** (setting and time) of a scene. What might prove more effective?

Can the **Position** (place in the structure) of a scene be altered? To where?

Are all of the **Characters** essential to a scene? Who might be left out? Who would you like to see added?

What lines of **Dialogue** can be deleted? Rearranged?

What **Scene Value** can be re-located to other **scenes** or **sequences**?

What **Information** do we gather from the *juxtaposition* of **images**?

What **Distribution of Information** in the **text** is the most crucial?

What **subtexts** do you "read" in a scene? How might additional **subtexts** be incorporated?

Identify a Scene's **Contrasts** and **Connections**.

Can you find **Dramatic Irony**? What are the **Ironies** within a **Scene**?

Are all the **Set-Ups** necessary?

What other **Set-Ups** would you have provided?

What additional **Physical Action** and/or **Physical Life** would you have directed?

Can a **Scene** begin later, and end earlier than it does?

Does a **Scene** need more time at its opening and/or more time at its ending?

What additional **Postproduction** elements would you like to *see* and/or *hear*? Why?

What other **Choices** would you make to advance the **value** of a scene?

How are **meaning**, **ideas**, and **themes** included without harm to the storytelling?

A colleague at the School of Visual Arts commended my "going wide before going deep." This has been my intention. By *my* going wide, *you* can quickly gain a good deal of skill and knowledge, and with ever-increasing experience, *you* can't help but begin to go deep. This is not to deny the many terrific texts with a "deep focus" on specific filmmaking disciplines. But you will discover that the books that — in one way or another — still manage to stay "wide" will inspire *you* to go "deep." The truth is that gaining knowledge demands steady movement wide and deep and wide and…

The design of *Setting Up Your Scenes* will help you in your preproduction, production, and postproduction searches:

What is my **Scene** about?

Can my **Location** in place and time be better?

Are all of my **Characters** essential?

Can the **Dialogue** be rearranged or simplified to advantage?

Where should I put the **Camera**?

What **Great Choices** can I make to enhance my scene through understatement?

How does my **Scene** fit into sequences, and the needs of the entire film?

As a teacher I've been reading a "wide" assortment of good texts on filmmaking over and over again each new school year. As I have gained additional experience with each passing year of working and teaching, I have realized something more from every re-reading. While the contents of the books have (obviously) remained the same, I encounter them anew, with an ever-broader perspective, and deeper insights. This is the main reason that I hold onto all of my books.

Experience is perhaps the best teacher: You can only get better at what you do if you keep at it; and your good books will get better too! There is always more to learn; and being a life-long student is necessary if you want to keep moving ahead. I have been a *student* of film for about forty-five years, while actually being paid for more than forty of them.

I hope that you'll continue your scene studies. For now, you can make use of *my* template to discover the Inner Workings of *Every* Film; I expect you'll develop your own inventive models.

I've always believed — it's been an incentive for me — artists owe an appreciation to earlier generations who labored in pursuit of excellence. That's one reason that I included films from much of the last half century. That appreciation is given life in each new work of caring craft, creativity, and integrity.

A 2004 retrospective of seventy-two-year-old artist Lee Bontecou's work inspired these concluding words by Michael Kimmelman in the *New York Times*: "[We are reminded] what it means not only to live a life richly, but also to make art, as all serious artists do, for its own sake, out of inner necessity, because that is really the only good reason to be an artist."

If you *must* be a filmmaker, do good work and share it!

FILM LIST (IN ALPHABETICAL ORDER)

The African Queen (1951)
Producers:
Sam Spiegel
John Woolf
Production Companies:
Horizon Pictures (II) [gb]
Romulus Films Ltd. [gb]
Distributors:
CBS/Fox [us] (USA) VHS
CBS/Fox [us] (USA) laserdisc
Continental Home Video [br] (Brazil) video
Fox Video [us] video
Independent Film Distributors Ltd. (IFD) [gb]
Magnetic Video [us] video
United Artists [us] (1951) (USA)

Atlantic City (1980)
Producers:
Dennis Hèroux
John Kemeny
Executive Producers:
Joseph Beaubien
Gabriel Boustiani
Production Companies:
International Cinema Corporation
Selta Films [fr]

Canadian Film Development Corporation (CFDC) [ca]
Cine-Neighbor, Inc. [ca]
Famous Players Limited
Merchant Films
Distributors:
LMP [br] (Brazil) VHS
LW Editora [br] (Brazil) DVD
Paramount Home Video [us] (USA) VHS
Paramount Pictures [us] (1981) (USA)
Roadshow Home Video [au] Australia) VHS

The Battle of Algiers
(*La Battaglia di Algeri*) (Arabic/French, 1965)
Producers:
Antonio Musu
Yacef Saadi
Production Companies:
Casbah
Igor Film [it]
Distributors:
Criterion Collection [us] (2004) (USA) (DVD)
Globo Video [br] (Brazil) (VHS)
Image Entertainment Inc. [us] (USA) (laserdisc)
Rialto Pictures LLC [us] (2004)
          (USA) (theatrical) (re-release)
Rizzoli (1967) (USA) (subtitled)

The Bridge on the River Kwai (1957)
Producers:
Sam Spiegel
Production Companies:
Columbia Pictures Corporation [us]
Horizon Pictures (II) [gb]
Distributors:
Columbia Pictures [us]
Columbia TriStar Film Distributors International [us] (1999)
(Argentina)
Columbia TriStar Home Video [us] (USA) DVD
Columbia TriStar Home Video [us] (USA) laserdisc
LK-TEL [ar] (1999) (Argentina) video
RCA/Columbia (USA) laserdisc

Burnt by the Sun (*Ultomlyonnye Solntsem*) (Russian, 1994)
Producers:
Michael Seydoux
Nikita Mikhalkov
Co-Producers:
Nicole Canne
Jean-Louis Pel
Vladimir Sedov
Executive Producer:
Leonid Vereshchagin
Production Companies:
Camera One [fr]

Le Studio Canal+ [fr]
Studio Trite
Distributors:
Araba Films [es] (Spain)
Columbia TriStar Home Video [us]
Mundial Films [ar] (Argentina)
Sony Pictures Classics [us]
Transeuropa Video Entertainment [ar]

Butch Cassidy and the Sundance Kid (1969)
Producers:
Paul Monash
John Foreman
Production Companies:
20th Century Fox [us]
Campanile
Distributors:
20th Century Fox Film Corporation [us]
20th Century Fox Home Entertainment [us] DVD
CBS/Fox [us] (USA) VHS
CBS/Fox [us] (USA) laserdisc
Encore (UK) laserdisc
Fox Home Entertainment [br] (Brazil) DVD
Fox Home Entertainment [br] (Brazil) VHS
Fox Video [us] laserdisc
Magnetic Video [us] video

Central Station (*Central do Brasil*) (Portuguese, 1998)
Producers:
Martine de Clermont-Tonnerre
Arthur Cohn
Associate Producer:
Paulo Carlos De Brito
Jack Gajos
Executive Producers:
Lillian Birnbaum
Thomas Garvin
Donald Ranvaud
Elisa Tolomelli
Production Companies:
Le Studio Canal+ [fr]
MACT Productions [fr]
Riofilmes [br]
Videofilms
Distributors:
Asociace Ceskych Filmovych Klubu (ACFK) [cz] (Czech Republic)
Buena Vista International (Germany) GmbH [de]
Buena Vista International [ar] (Argentina)
EDKO Film Ltd. [hk] (Hong Kong)
Europa Carat [br] (Brazil) VHS
Europa Filmes [br] (Brazil) DVD
Filmes Lusomundo [pt] (Portugal)
Gativideo [ar] (Argentina) video
Home Vision Entertainment (HVE) [us] (2004) (USA) DVD

RCV Film Distribution [ni] (Belgium)
RCV Film Distribution [ni] (Luxembourg)
RCV Film Distribution [ni] (Netherlands)
Sony Pictures Classics [us] (USA) (subtitled)

Children of a Lesser God (1986)
Producers:
Burt Sugarman
Patrick Palmer
Production Company:
Paramount Pictures [us]
Distributors:
Argentina Video Home (AVH) [ar] Argentina DVD
Argentina Video Home (AVH) [ar] Argentina VHS
CIC Video [br] (Brazil) VHS
CIC-Taft Home Video [au]
Paramount Home Video [us] (USA) laserdisc
Paramount Pictures [us]
United International Pictures (UIP) [ar] (2004)
        (Argentina) re-release

Chinatown (1974)
Producer:
Robert Evans
Associate Producer:
C.O. Erickson
Production Company:
Long Road
Paramount Pictures [us]
Penthouse
Distributors:
C.I.C. (Consorcio Ibérico Cinematográfico) [es] (Spain)
CIC-Taft Home Video [au] Australia VHS
Paramount Home Video [us] (USA) DVD
Paramount Home Video [us] (USA) VHS
Paramount Home Video [us] (USA) laserdisc
Paramount Pictures [us]
Prem'er Video Fil'm [ru] (Russia) VHS

Cinema Paradiso (*Nuovo cinema Paradiso*) (Italian, 1989)
Producers:
Mino Barbera
Franco Cristaldi
Giovanna Romagnoli
Production Companies:
Cristaldifilm
Les Films Ariane [fr]

Radiotelevisione Italiana (RAI) [it]
TF1 Films Productions [fr]
Distributors:
Home Box Office (HBO) Home Video [us] (USA) DVD
Columbia TriStar [br] (Brazil) VHS
Miramax Films [us] (1990) (USA) (subtitled)
Miramax Films [us] (2002) (USA) (theatrical)
        (re-release) (director's cut)
Miramax Home Entertainment [us] (2003) (USA) DVD
Nippon Herald Films [jp] (Japan)
Spentzos Films [gr] (Greece) VHS
Transmundo Films [ar] (Argentina)
Transmundo Home Video (THV) [ar] (Argentina) video
Versàtil Home Video [br] (Brazil) DVD

Colonel Redl (*Oberst Redl*) (German, 1985)
Producer:
József Marx
Production Companies:
MAFILM Objektív Filmstúdió [hu]
MOKEP-Kerzi
Manfred Durniok Filmproduktion [de]
Zweites Deutsches Fernsehen (ZDF) [de]
Österreichischer Rundfunk (ORF) [at]
Distributors:
Anchor Bay Entertainment [us] (USA) DVD
Orion Classics [us] (USA) subtitled

The Day of the Jackal (1973)
Producer:
John Woolf
Co-Producers:
Julien Derode
David Deutsch
Production Companies:
Universal Productions France S.A. [fr]
Warwick Film Productions Ltd. [gb]
Distributors:
CIC Video [br] (Brazil) VHS
Columbia TriStar [br] (Brazil) DVD
MCA/Universal Home Video [us] (USA) VHS
MCA/Universal Home Video [us] (USA) laserdisc
MCA/Universal Pictures [us]
Universal Home Entertainment [us] (USA) DVD

Death in Venice (*Morte a Venezia*) (Italian, 1971)
Producer:
Luchino Visconti
Production Company:
Alfa Cinematografica [it]
Distributors:
Warner Bros. [us] (1971) world wide theatrical.
Warner Home Video [us] world wide VHS
Associate Ceskych Filmovych Klubu

(ACFK) [cz] (Czech Republic)
Warner Home Video [us] 2004 (USA) DVD
Warner Home Video [br] (Brazil) VHS

Dial M for Murder (1954)
Producer:
Alfred Hitchcock
Production Company:
Warner Bros. [us]
Distributors:
Sociedade Importadora de Filmes (SIF) [pt] (Portugal)
Warner Bros. [us]
Warner Home Video [us] (USA) VHS
Warner Home Video [us] (USA) laserdisc
Warner Home Video [br] (Brazil) VHS

Dog Day Afternoon (1975)
Producers:
Martin Bregman
Martin Elfand
Associate Producer:
Robert Greenhut
Production Company:
Artists Entertainment Complex

Distributors:
Varus Video [ru]
Warner Bros. [us]
Warner Home Video [br] (Brazil) DVD
Warner Home Video [br] (Brazil) VHS

Fanny & Alexander (*Fanny och Alexander*) (Swedish, 1982)
Producers:
Jörn Donner
Daniel Toscan du Plantier
Co-Producer:
Renzo Rossellini
Production Companies:
Cinematograph AB [se]
Gaumont International [fr]
Opera Film Produzione [it]
Personafilm
SVT Drama [se]
Sandrews [se]
Svenska Filminstitutet (SFI) [se]
TVI
Tobis Filmkunst [de]
Distributors:
Artificial Eye [gb]
Embassy Pictures Corporation [us] (1983) (USA) subtitled
Ifa Argentina (Argentina)

Pole Vídeo Comunicacões Ltda. [br] (Brazil) VHS
Sandrew [se]
Versátil Home Video [br] (Brazil) DVD

The Four Hundred Blows
(*Les quatre cents coups*) (French, 1959)
Producers:
François Truffaut
Production Companies:
Les Films du Carrosse [fr]
Sédif Productions [fr]
Distributors:
Altomedia. Co. Ltd. [kr] (Korea) (DVD)
ClassicLine [br] (Brazil) (DVD)
Cocinor [fr]
Fox Lorber [us] (USA) (DVD)
Rosebud [gr] (Greece) (theatrical re-release)
Zenith International (USA) (subtitled)

The French Connection (1971)
Producers:
Philip D'Antoni
Executive Producer:
G. David Shine

Associate Producer:
Kenneth UttG.
Production Companies:
20th Century Fox [us]
D'Antoni Productions
Schine-Moore Productions [us]
Distributor:
20th Century Fox Film Corporation [us]

Hiroshima Mon Amour (French, 1959)
Producers:
Anatole Dauman
Samy Halfon
Production Companies:
Argos Films [fr]
Como
Daiei Studios [jp]
Pathè Entertainment
Distributors:
Cocinor [fr]
Criterion Collection [us] DVD
Reel Media International [us] (USA)
Sagres Filmes [br] (Brazil) VHS
Zenith International (1960) (USA) subtitled

Jean de Florette (French, 1986)
Producer:
Pierre Grunstein
Production Companies:
DD Productions [fr]
Films A2 [fr]
Rai Due Radiotelevisione Italiana [it]
Renn Productions [fr]
Tèlèvision Suisse-Romande (TSR) [ch]
Distributors:
Orion Classics [us] (1987) (USA) subtitled
Transmundo Films [ar] (Argentina)
Transmundo Home Video (THV) [ar] (Argentina) video

Ju Dou (Chinese, 1990)
Producers:
Hu Jian, Yasuyoshi Tokuma & Wenze Zhang
Production Companies:
China Film Co-Production Corporation
China Film Release Import & Export Company
Tokuma Shoten
Xi'an Film Studio
Distributors:
Film Arte (Argentina)
Miramax Films (USA)
Transeuropa Video Entertainment (Argentina)

Kolya (Czech, 1996)
Producers:
Eric Abraham & Jan Sveràk
Co-Producer:
Jiri Sveràk
Production Companies:
Biograf Jan Sverak
Centre National de la Cinèmatographie (CNC) [fr]
CinemArt [cz]
Czech TV [cz]
Eurimages
Pandora Cinema [us]
Portobello Pictures [gb]
Space Films
Distributors:
Argentina Video Home (AVH) [ar]
Buena Vista International (Germany) GmbH [de]
Buena Vista International Spain S.A. [es] Spain
Buena Vista International [us]
Eurocine [ar] (Argentina)
Gaumont Buena Vista International (GBVI) [fr] (France)
Miramax Films [us] 1997 (USA)
Miramax Films [us] 1997 (USA)
Space Films [cz] (Czech Republic)
Versàtil Home Video [br] (Brazil) DVD
Warner Home Video [br] (Brazil) VHS

Léolo (French, 1992)
Producers:
Aimée Danis
Lyse Lafontainey
Co-Producers:
Jean-Francois Lepetit
Isabelle Fauvel
Executive Producers:
Robert Lantos
Claudette Viau
Production Companies:
Aliance Films Corporation
Center National de la Cinématographie (CNC) [fr]
Flach Film [fr]
La Ministre de la Culture et de la Communication
La Procirep
La Societe de Radio-Television Quebec [ca]
Le Studio Canal+ [fr]
Les Productions du Verseau [ca]
National Film Board of Canada (NFB) [ca]
Super Ècran [ca]
Téléfilm Canada [ca]
Distributors:
Alta Films S.A. [es] (Spain)
Fine Line Features [us]

The Little Fugitive (1953)
Producers:
Ray Ashley & Morris Engel
Production Company:
Little Fugitive Production Company [us]
Distributors:
Joseph Burstyn Inc. [us]
Kino Video [us] (USA) DVD
Kino Video [us] (USA) VHS

My Beautiful Laundrette (1985)
Producers:
Tim Bevan & Sarah Radclyffe
Production Companies:
Channel Four Films [gb]
SAF Productions [gb]
Working Title Films [gb]
Distributors:
Mainline Pictures [gb] (1985) (UK)
Mundial Filmes [br] (Brazil) video
Orion Classics [us] (1986) (USA)

Rosemary's Baby (1968)
Producer:
William Castle
Associate Producer:
Donna Holloway
Production Company:
Paramount Pictures [us]
Distributors:
CIC-Taft Home Video [au]
Paramount Home Video [us] (USA) DVD
Paramount Home Video [us] (USA) laserdisc
Paramount Pictures [us]
RCA/Columbia Pictures Home Video [us] (USA) VHS
Renacimiento [ar] (Argentina) video

Seven Beauties (*Pasqualino Settebellezze*) (Italian, 1976)
Producers:
Arrigo Colombo & Lina Wertmüller
Production Company:
Medusa Produzione [it]
Distributors:
Cinema 5 Distributing [us] (USA) (theatrical) (dubbed)
Fox Lorber [us] (USA) DVD
Warner Brothers [us] (theatrical) (non-USA)

The Shop on Main Street (*Obchod na korze*) (Czech, 1965)
Producers:
Jordan Balurov
M. Broz
Karel Feix
Jaromír Lukás
Production Company:
Filmovè Studio Barrandov [cshh]
Distributors:
Asociace Ceskych Filmovych Klubu (ACFK) [cz] (Czech Republic)
Criterion Collection [us] DVD
Prominent Films (1966) (USA) (subtitled)

Sophie's Choice (1982)
Producer:
Keith Barish & Alan Pakula
Executive Producer:
Martin Starger
Production Company:
Incorporated Television Company (ITC) [gb]
Distributors:
Associated Film Distribution [us]
Editora Europa [br] (Brazil) DVD
Universal Pictures [us]
Versàtil Home Video [br] (Brazil) DVD
Versàtil Home Video [br] (Brazil) VHS

Three Days of the Condor (1975)
Producer:
Stanley Schneider
Executive Producer:
Dino De Laurentiis
Production Companies:
Dino De Laurnetiis Corporation [us]
Paramount Pictures [us]
Wildwood Enterprises [us]
Distributors:
Hafbo (Netherlands)
Paramount Home Video [us] (DVD)
Paramount Pictures [us]
Tec Home Video [br] (Brazil) (Video)
Video Classics

Tom Jones (1963)
Producer:
Tony Richardson
Associate Producers:
Michael Holden; Oscar Lewenstein
Executive Producer:
Michael Balcon
Production Company:
Woodfall Film Productions [GB]
Distributors:
Lopert Pictures Corporation [US]
Samuel Goldwyn Company [US]
United Artists [US]

The Treasure of the Sierra Madre (1948)
Executive Producer:
Jack L. Warner
Producers:
Henry Blanke
Production Company:
Warner Brothers [us]
Distributors:
Elite Films [es]
Key Video [us] (video)
MGM/UA Home Entertainment Inc. [us] (video)
Warner Brothers [us]
Warner Home Video [us] (2003) (USA) (DVD)
Warner Home Video [br] (Brazil) (VHS)

Two Women (*La Ciociara*) (Italian, 1960)
Producer:
Carlo Ponti
Executive Producer:
Joseph E. Levine
Production Company:
Compagnia Cinematografica Champon [it]
Les Films Marceau-Cocinor [fr]
Sociètè Gènèrale de Cinèmatographie
Distributors:
Embassy Pictures Corporation [us] 1961 (USA)

The Verdict (1983)
Producers:
David Brown
Richard D. Zanuck
Executive Producer:
Burt Harris
Production Company:
20th Century Fox
Distributors:
20th Century Fox Film Corporation, U.S.A.
20th Century Fox Home Entertainment, U.S.A.
Abril Video, Brazil
CBS/Fox, U.S.A.

The White Balloon (*Badkanake Sefid*) (Farsi, 1995)
Producer:
Kurosh Mazkouri
Production Company:
Ferdou Films
Distributors:
Civite Films S.L. (Spain)
IFA (Argentina)
Kidmark, A Division of Trimark Entertainment (Video)
October Films, U.S. 1996

ABOUT THE AUTHOR

Photo by David Dessel

Richard D. Pepperman lives in Monmouth County, NJ, and Mount Holly, VT.

CREDITS INCLUDE:

Co-Editor: *The Boy From New Orleans: A Tribute To Louis Armstrong.*

Editor: *Touch: The Domain Of The Senses.* Official Entry, Sitges Film Festival.

Consulting Editor: *Five Wives, Three Secretaries & Me.* Honored by the Academy Of Motion Picture Arts & Sciences as one of the Outstanding Documentaries of 1999.

Consulting Editor: *Say It Isn't So.* Official Entry, Rotterdam Film Festival.

Production/Postproduction Advisor: *Echoes.* Official Entry, Munich Film Festival.
Karlovy Vary Film Festival.

Screenwriting Judge: Nicholl Fellowships; Academy Of Motion Picture Arts & Sciences.

Supervising Editor: Promotional Music Videos, Columbia Records, *The Music People.*

Editor on more than 1000 commercial spots, including Postproduction Supervisor, *Barrier Free Design*: PSA Spot; Andy Award.

Designed and conducted editing workshops and seminars at Film/Video Arts, Pratt Institute, and The New School University.

Author of *The Eye is Quicker. Film Editing: Making A Good Film Better* (Michael Wiese Productions, 2004).

Richard is a teacher and thesis advisor at the School of Visual Arts, where he was honored with the Distinguished Artist-Teacher Award.

RICHARD D. PEPPERMAN

Consulting | Editing | Supervision | Consulting | Editing | Supervision

Consulting | Editing | Supervision | Consulting | Editing | Supervision

Consulting | Editing | Supervision | Consulting | Editing | Supervision

Consulting | Editing | Supervision | Consulting | Editing | Supervision

Consulting | Editing | Supervision | Consulting | Editing | Supervision

Consulting | Editing | Supervision | Consulting | Editing | Supervision

FOR MORE INFORMATION ON THESE SERVICES PLEASE CONTACT RICHARD D. PEPPERMAN : *rdpEditor@juno.com*

SETTING UP YOUR SHOTS
GREAT CAMERA MOVES EVERY FILMMAKER SHOULD KNOW

JEREMY VINEYARD

BEST SELLER
OVER 27,300 UNITS SOLD!

Written in straightforward, non-technical language and laid out in a nonlinear format with self-contained chapters for quick, on-the-set reference, *Setting Up Your Shots* is like a Swiss army knife for filmmakers! Using examples from over 140 popular films, this book provides detailed descriptions of more than 100 camera setups, angles, and techniques — in an easy-to-use horizontal "wide-screen" format.

Setting Up Your Shots is an excellent primer for beginning filmmakers and students of film theory, as well as a handy guide for working filmmakers. If you are a director, a storyboard artist, or an animator, use this book. It is the culmination of hundreds of hours of research.

Contains 150 references to the great shots from your favorite films, including *2001: A Space Odyssey*, *Blue Velvet*, *The Matrix*, *The Usual Suspects*, and *Vertigo*.

"Perfect for any film enthusiast looking for the secrets behind creating film. Because of its simplicity of design and straightforward storyboards, Setting Up Your Shots is destined to be mandatory reading at film schools throughout the world."
— Ross Otterman, Directed By Magazine

"Setting Up Your Shots is a great book for defining the shots of today. The storyboard examples on every page make it a valuable reference book for directors and DPs alike! This great learning tool should be a boon for writers who want to choose the most effective shot and clearly show it in their boards for the maximum impact."
— Paul Clatworthy, Creator, StoryBoard Artist and StoryBoard Quick Software

"This book is for both beginning and experienced filmmakers. It's a great reference tool, a quick reminder of the most commonly used shots by the greatest filmmakers of all time."
— Cory Williams, President, Alternative Productions

SETTING UP YOUR SHOTS
Great Camera Moves Every Filmmaker Should Know
By Jeremy Vineyard · Illustrated by Jose Cruz

JEREMY VINEYARD is a filmmaker, internationally published author, and screenwriter. He is currently assembling a cast and crew for a crime feature to be shot in 2005.

$19.95 | 132 PAGES

ORDER # 8RLS | ISBN: 0-941188-73-6

MICHAEL WIESE PRODUCTIONS

Since 1981, Michael Wiese Productions has been dedicated to providing both novice and seasoned filmmakers with vital information on all aspects of filmmaking. We have published more than 70 books, used in over 500 film schools and countless universities, and by hundreds of thousands of filmmakers worldwide.

Our authors are successful industry professionals who spend innumerable hours writing about the hard stuff: budgeting, financing, directing, marketing, and distribution. They believe that if they share their knowledge and experience with others, more high quality films will be produced.

And that has been our mission, now complemented through our new web-based resources. We invite all readers to visit www.mwp.com to receive free tipsheets and sample chapters, participate in forum discussions, obtain product discounts — and even get the opportunity to receive free books, project consulting, and other services offered by our company.

Our goal is, quite simply, to help you reach your goals. That's why we give our readers the most complete portal for filmmaking knowledge available — in the most convenient manner.

We truly hope that our books and web-based resources will empower you to create enduring films that will last for generations to come.

Let us hear from you at anytime.

Sincerely,
Michael Wiese
Publisher, Filmmaker

www.mwp.com

FILM & VIDEO BOOKS

Alone In a Room: *Secrets of Successful Screenwriters*
John Scott Lewinski / $19.95

Cinematic Storytelling: *The 100 Most Powerful Film Conventions Every Filmmaker Must Know* / Jennifer Van Sijll / $22.95

The Complete Independent Movie Marketing Handbook: *Promote, Distribute & Sell Your Film or Video* / Mark Steven Bosko / $39.95

Costume Design 101: *The Art and Business of Costume Design for Film and Television* / Richard La Motte / $19.95

Could It Be a Movie? *How to Get Your Ideas Out of Your Head and Up on the Screen* / Christina Hamlett / $26.95

Crashing Hollywood: *How to Keep Your Integrity Up, Your Clothes On & Still Make It in Hollywood* / Fran Harris / $24.95

Creating Characters: *Let Them Whisper Their Secrets*
Marisa D'Vari / $26.95

The Crime Writer's Reference Guide: *1001 Tips for Writing the Perfect Murder*
Martin Roth / $17.95

Cut by Cut: *Editing Your Film or Video*
Gael Chandler / $35.95

Cut to the Chase: *Forty-Five Years of Editing America's Favorite Movies*
Sam O'Steen as told to Bobbie O'Steen / $24.95

Digital Cinema: *The Hollywood Insider's Guide to the Evolution of Storytelling*
Thom Taylor and Melinda Hsu / $27.95

Digital Editing with Final Cut Pro 4 *(includes 45 minutes of DVD tutorials and sample footage)* / Bruce Mamer and Jason Wallace / $31.95

Digital Filmmaking 101: *An Essential Guide to Producing Low-Budget Movies*
Dale Newton and John Gaspard / $24.95

Digital Moviemaking, 2nd Edition: *All the Skills, Techniques, and Moxie You'll Need to Turn Your Passion into a Career* / Scott Billups / $26.95

Directing Actors: *Creating Memorable Performances for Film and Television*
Judith Weston / $26.95

Directing Feature Films: *The Creative Collaboration Between Directors, Writers, and Actors* / Mark Travis / $26.95

Dream Gear: *Cool & Innovative Tools for Film, Video & TV Professionals*
Catherine Lorenze / $29.95

The Encyclopedia of Underground Movies: *Films from the Fringes of Cinema*
Phil Hall / $26.95

The Eye is Quicker *Film Editing: Making a Good Film Better*
Richard D. Pepperman / $27.95

Film & Video Budgets, 3rd Updated Edition
Deke Simon and Michael Wiese / $26.95

Film Directing: *Cinematic Motion, 2nd Edition*
Steven D. Katz / $27.95

Film Directing: *Shot by Shot, Visualizing from Concept to Screen*
Steven D. Katz / $27.95

The Film Director's Intuition: *Script Analysis and Rehearsal Techniques*
Judith Weston / $26.95

Film Production Management 101: *The Ultimate Guide for Film and Television Production Management and Coordination* / Deborah S. Patz / $39.95

Filmmaking for Teens: *Pulling Off Your Shorts*
Troy Lanier and Clay Nichols / $18.95

First Time Director: *How to Make Your Breakthrough Movie*
Gil Bettman / $27.95

From Word to Image: *Storyboarding and the Filmmaking Process*
Marcie Begleiter / $26.95

The Hollywood Standard: *The Complete & Authoritative Guide to Script Format and Style* / Christopher Riley / $18.95

The Independent Film and Videomakers Guide, 2nd Edition: *Expanded and Updated* / Michael Wiese / $29.95

Inner Drives: *How to Write & Create Characters Using the Eight Classic Centers of Motivation* / Pamela Jaye Smith / $26.95

Joe Leydon's Guide to Essential Movies You Must See: *If You Read, Write About – or Make Movies* / Joe Leydon / $24.95

Myth and the Movies: *Discovering the Mythic Structure of 50 Unforgettable Films* / Stuart Voytilla / $26.95

On the Edge of a Dream: *Magic & Madness in Bali*
Michael Wiese / $16.95

The Perfect Pitch: *How to Sell Yourself and Your Movie Idea to Hollywood*
Ken Rotcop / $16.95

Psychology for Screenwriters: *Building Conflict in your Script*
William Indick, Ph.D. / $26.95

Save the Cat! *The Last Book on Screenwriting You'll Ever Need*
Blake Snyder / $19.95

Screenwriting 101: *The Essential Craft of Feature Film Writing*
Neill D. Hicks / $16.95

Script Partners: *What Makes Film and TV Writing Teams Work*
Claudia Johnson and Matt Stevens / $24.95

The Script-Selling Game: *A Hollywood Insider's Look at Getting Your Script Sold and Produced* / Kathie Fong Yoneda / $14.95

Setting Up Your Shots: *Great Camera Moves Every Filmmaker Should Know*
Jeremy Vineyard / $19.95

Shaking the Money Tree, 2nd Edition: *How to Get Grants and Donations for Film and Television* / Morrie Warshawski / $26.95

Sound Design: *The Expressive Power of Music, Voice, and Sound Effects in Cinema* / David Sonnenschein / $19.95

Stealing Fire From the Gods: *A Dynamic New Story Model for Writers and Filmmakers* / James Bonnet / $26.95

Storyboarding 101: *A Crash Course in Professional Storyboarding*
James O. Fraioli / $19.95

The Ultimate Filmmaker's Guide to Short Films: *Making It Big in Shorts*
Kim Adelman / $14.95

What Are You Laughing At? *How to Write Funny Screenplays, Stories, and More*
Brad Schreiber / $19.95

The Working Director: *How to Arrive, Thrive & Survive in the Director's Chair*
Charles Wilkinson / $22.95

The Writer's Journey, 2nd Edition: *Mythic Structure for Writers*
Christopher Vogler / $24.95

The Writer's Partner: *1001 Breakthrough Ideas to Stimulate Your Imagination*
Martin Roth / $19.95

Writing the Action Adventure: *The Moment of Truth*
Neill D. Hicks / $14.95

Writing the Comedy Film: *Make 'Em Laugh*
Stuart Voytilla and Scott Petri / $14.95

Writing the Fantasy Film: *Heroes and Journeys in Alternate Realities*
Sable Jak / $26.95

Writing the Killer Treatment: *Selling Your Story Without a Script*
Michael Halperin / $14.95

Writing the Second Act: *Building Conflict and Tension in Your Film Script*
Michael Halperin / $19.95

Writing the Thriller Film: *The Terror Within*
Neill D. Hicks / $14.95

DVD & VIDEOS

Hardware Wars: *DVD*
Written and Directed by Ernie Fosselius / $14.95

Hardware Wars: *Special Edition VHS Video*
Written and Directed by Ernie Fosselius / $9.95

Field of Fish: *VHS Video*
Directed by Steve Tanner and Michael Wiese, Written by Annamaria Murphy / $9.95